HEALTHY
HYPNOSIS

Simple Truth and Practical Use

by Paul Gustafson R.N., C.H.

Healthy Hypnosis – Simple Truth and Practical Use
© 2010 by Paul Gustafson

The information contained in this book is intended to be educational and not for diagnosis, prescription, or treatment of any health disorder whatsoever. This information should not replace consultation with a competent healthcare professional. The content of the book is intended to be used as an adjunct to a rational and responsible healthcare program. The author and publisher are in no way liable for any misuse of the material.

Printed in the United States of America.

Book Design and Layout by Picturia Press
www.picturiapress.com

INTRODUCTION

Before I started writing this book I wanted to check out the competition. I figured there couldn't be too many hypnosis-obsessed individuals like me writing books, so I Googled "hypnosis books" and was shocked to see that there are 2.72 million listings. You would think I would have found something else to do with my time after such a discovery but apparently I have something to say on the subject and need to be heard.

After being in practice for ten years I would say the aspect of hypnosis that amazes and excites me the most is how rapidly positive change can be achieved. Individuals walk into my office with the weight of the world on their shoulders and after the first session they notice a shift.

I also think that what distinguishes my hypnosis skill set from most other hypnotists is not only my background as a registered nurse (nurses make the best hypnotists) but my extensive experience as a hospice nurse. There is a very small window of opportunity to get to know our patients, develop their trust, and produce solutions to their problems. These skills translate beautifully into hypnosis but the hospice component takes it to a whole new level. Nurse hypnotists with a hospice background are empathic, active listeners; from this they develop productive rapport, which greatly enhances the positive results with hypnosis.

In my hypnosis practice it usually takes only about ten minutes to go from our initial meeting to hearing the client's deepest darkest secrets. The other aspect that might set me apart from most involves time. Although I am certainly as interested in making a living as the next guy, I never rush anyone out the door to make room for the next client. I've heard stories of how some hypnotists see 10-15 clients/day, and how others even deceive their clients by playing pre-recorded sessions rather than conducting the sessions live.

One of the first rules you learn in hospice is to listen, and when you think it is time to speak, listen some more. This philosophy is pivotal in hypnosis as well. When someone feels as though they are being heard they feel supported and let down their guard, which enables them to transition into productive levels of hypnotic trance.

When I first became a certified hypnotist I recall thinking how familiar hypnosis felt to me. Even though I had never formally hypnotized anyone prior to my training, I felt as though I had been doing this work all along.

My first experience with hypnosis was as an overwhelmed, stressed-out teenager. Even at an early age I was concerned about taking medications, and wanted to find a non-pharmacological solution. I found a local hypnotist in the phone book and made an appointment. I clearly remember his bare-bones office, sparsely furnished with only a small desk and a couple of metal chairs. He was an older man, perhaps in his early 70's, with a very soft, comforting voice. After a brief discussion about my problems and how hypnosis worked, he asked me to look up at the ceiling.

He quietly spoke about how easy it was to settle into hypnosis. He explained that I would begin to experience a flow of warm relaxation that would spread from my toes up through my body. When it reached my eyes, they would close and I would go into deep hypnotic trance. He was right; I quickly slipped into a new and wonderful state of mind.

Under hypnosis, I felt completely free of all stress, worry, or concern. As I basked in this newfound euphoria, he asked me to imagine a scenario I usually found very stressful. He asked me to picture it as though I were a movie director with the authority to make any changes I desired. As I pictured circumstances that normally paralyzed me with anxiety, I experienced feelings of confident success instead.

I'll never forget how I felt after that session. It was as though I had morphed into an enhanced, optimized version of myself. I felt grounded, calm, and very sure of myself. The hypnotist recorded the session and handed me a cassette tape to listen to on my own. I was able to listen to the tape as often as I wished. I only had a few sessions with that gentleman, but the impression he made eventually led to something very special.

Years later, when I was in college, hypnosis made another dramatic entrance into my life. I had to make a presentation that represented a significant portion of my grade. I had always had difficulty with public speaking, so I decided to revisit hypnosis. I was fortunate enough to locate a psychologist who used hypnosis as part of her practice.

She conducted three hypnosis sessions that focused on my fears about public speaking. Like the hypnotist I had visited during my teens, she also recorded the sessions. I then had four weeks to absorb the hypnotic messages for speaking success. It was a very interesting process because initially my inner voice worked hard to hold onto my irrational fears. With repetition, however, a new wave of focused confidence eventually dissolved my anxieties.

Without hypnosis, I would have been anticipating failure. Instead, I felt relaxed and ready. I was amazed at how well I slept the night before my presentation. After I woke, I continued to feel surprisingly calm and found myself thinking of anything but the presentation as I drove to class that day.

Prior to learning how to use hypnosis, public speaking, even in front of a small group, made me feel like a ticking bomb about to explode. That day I was comfortably at ease listening to class-mates make their presentations. When I heard my name called, I stood and began to walk calmly toward the podium.

At that moment I was of two minds. I certainly had a conscious memory of my past difficulties with public speaking, but as I began my presentation, there seemed to be something stronger at work. The experience was quite surreal, as though I had entered a state of mind similar to the calm I usually felt during the hypnosis sessions I had been diligently listening to for the previous four weeks.

I remember thinking, "This is strange; I haven't exploded yet and I seem to be speaking." As I gave my presentation, I comfortably transitioned from anticipating crisis to a feeling of confident competence. This positive experience forever bonded me to the power of hypnosis. It was then that I realized how, with just a little guidance, we can overcome and succeed in areas we never thought possible.

Through the years that followed, I continued using self-hypnosis. If I felt overwhelmed, I frequently used the image of riding downward in an elevator with a glass door. As it carried me into relaxation, I imagined that the floors represented my problems. By descending beneath the problems, I envisioned becoming free of them. This was a very effective technique that I still use with many of my clients.

Eventually, my professional work focused on acute care and hospice nursing. In fact, during my time in hospice I learned how to listen, connect, and communicate in meaningful ways with my patients and their families. These skills translated nicely into my work as a hypnotist.

Once I decided to change my career path into hypnosis, things progressed very quickly. I was fortunate to be a guest on a major Boston radio station. After that exposure, a local television station decided to do a program on hypnosis, which I also participated in. Both of these experiences dramatically increased my business and eventually inspired me to produce and host my own cable television show. I often recall how my experience with that old hypnotist so long ago evolved into a career filled with enjoyable challenges, creative opportunities, and personal fulfillment.

TABLE OF CONTENTS

WHAT IS HYPNOSIS

Unfortunately, hypnosis has been buried under decades of myth, misconception, and manipulation. It has been one of the most misunderstood of the complementary sciences. Over the years, however, the accumulation of positive scientific research has become too great to ignore.

Here is a list of some reputable hypnosis research organizations:

- American Society of Clinical Hypnosis
  http://www.asch.net/

- Society for Clinical and Experimental Hypnosis
  http://www.sceh.us/index.htm

- International Journal of Clinical and Experimental Hypnosis
  http://ijceh.educ.wsu.edu

- American Psychological Association: Division 30, Psychological Hypnosis
  http://www.apa.org/divisions/div30/

Hypnosis is now consistently validated as one of the leading therapeutic tools for personal positive change. Today's practicing hypnotists have benefited from all of the dedicated research conducted by these fine organizations.

Knowledge is power for practitioner and client alike. Research certainly helps me better understand the science of hypnosis, which in turn helps me provide better treatment to my clients. Individuals who understand how hypnosis works and how to use it productively are more likely to achieve their goals.

I describe hypnosis as a daydream on demand. During hypnosis, we go to the same brain state as when we zone out, meditate, practice guided imagery, or experience progressive relaxation. These are all states in which the subconscious mind becomes receptive. With hypnosis, the goal is to positively empower an individual's inner thoughts to support their conscious desires.

Imagine that wonderful feeling that we all experience during a deep daydream, when we don't have a care in the world. It feels as if a layer of comforting insulation is shielding us from the stressful assembly line of life. The reason daydreams feel different from our usual reality is because during them, the subconscious becomes more open and active than it normally is.

We are all hard-wired with the ability to access the subconscious mind and long-term memory. Unfortunately, until we learn about hypnosis, usually the only time we experience this state is while staring mindlessly at a television or computer screen, waiting in line at the grocery store, or on a long drive.

The reason it is so helpful to enter this brain state is because it is where we store all of our life experiences, habits, patterns, values, and beliefs. By deliberately accessing the subconscious, two important goals can be accomplished: We can remove unproductive values, habits, or beliefs, and we can replace them with preferred alternatives. With hypnosis, the connection to past problems can be quickly severed, thereby freeing one to establish a new life path.

You go to the physical gym to increase your stamina and strength. Why not go to the mental gym to positively enhance your thoughts and perception? The repetition of physical exercise tones and strengthens our bodies, just as the repetition of hypnosis establishes and solidifies positive change.

As a hypnotist, I teach individuals to relax in a particular way and then guide them into the depths of subconscious thought, where dreams manifest into a new reality. Clients apply meaning to the messages I give them in whatever manner works best for them. Some people connect more with the words they hear, while others create vivid imagery during the trance state. Enabling clients to understand this simple truth helps them own the hypnotic process, which further empowers them to shape the lives they choose to live.

To those who doubt that they can be hypnotized, I ask if they like the idea of becoming so powerfully relaxed that they can easily establish positive change. Who could resist such a notion? If an individual has difficulty entering into hypnosis, it is more likely due to inadequate preparation or faulty technique on the part of the hypnotist.

Another significant part of the process is rapport. Effective sessions require a relationship of trust and cooperation with the client. If clients feel comfortable with the process and the practitioner, and also value the suggestions they receive during a session, success usually follows.

Even those who know nothing about hypnosis are aware that we all have short-term and long-term memory. The short-term memory is the conscious mind, and the long-term memory is the subconscious mind. The conscious mind is the more active of the two. It is the gatekeeper. It analyzes and judges, accepting or denying the storage of information in the subconscious mind.

The subconscious mind is a complex and powerful place. Think of it as our storage and control center. It is also the home of our imagination. The subconscious is active when we daydream, zone out, watch television, and when we sleep. It is also active when we're hypnotized. When clients understand that entering into hypnosis is something we are all familiar with, the process is easier and more productive.

WILL I GIVE UP FREE WILL?

The fear of relinquishing free will while hypnotized stems from a very common misconception that couldn't be further from the truth. Hypnosis actually helps individuals tap into powerful inner resources they never knew they had. If a session is not in line with one's values and beliefs, the client will reject the experience entirely. Not only does the hypnotist have to offer sessions of value, but the phraseology and technique need to be just right for a positive connection between client and patient to occur.

For those concerned about mind control, a more relevant concern might be the insidious manipulation of advertising. As previously mentioned, we all go into a light hypnotic trance every time we stare at a television screen. While the conscious mind is taking a break, what we are viewing is more likely to be subconsciously filed away. Considering the nature of advertising and the content of television programming in general, the actions we take as a result may not be in our best interest.

A.C. Nielsen says the average American watches more than four hours of television per day. In a span of 65 years, that adds up to nine years of tube time. Perhaps it's not surprising, therefore, that a Time magazine study revealed that today's children believe that fast food is healthier than a home-cooked meal. (*Time* 2004)

WHAT DOES HYPNOSIS FEEL LIKE?

The experience of hypnosis not only varies from person to person, but even for each individual from session to session. It is a unique combination of deep physical relaxation and heightened awareness. Many describe a soothing feeling of heaviness in their arms or legs, or they may feel as though they are sinking into the surface beneath them. Others describe sensations of floating.

As clients progress from session to session, they develop increased hypnotic skill. Some report a sensation of complete mind-body separation, as though they have lost awareness of their physical being.

Individuals also frequently experience profound clarity or resolution concerning problems that previously seemed complex or overwhelming. Through hypnosis, clients often find solutions to problems that are unrelated to the specific problem they intended to solve.

Most individuals hear and remember everything that is said to them during hypnosis, although occasionally some may dip so deeply into subconscious thought that they do not consciously hear or recall segments of the session. This is not a problem, because the subconscious always absorbs everything of value.

Those who happen to doze off during a hypnosis session still experience therapeutic benefits. As previously mentioned, the subconscious is open and active when we are hypnotized, and also when sleeping. When we sleep, the conscious mind sleeps. During hypnosis, however, the conscious mind is just less active than when we are awake, quietly monitoring things from the background.

A majority of my clients with demanding schedules find that bed-time is the only time available for listening to their home reinforcement recordings. I believe, however, that the best time of day to listen is in the morning. After a full night's sleep, individuals seem to engage more fully with the session. The time spent practicing hypnosis will also start their day with a burst of positive energy, clarity, and enthusiasm.

In my office there is a small sofa as well as a recliner. When a client comes in for their initial office visit, they usually sit on the sofa, as it is closer to the entrance. This is when they share the details of their problem. The pre-talk is not only helpful to the practitioner, but it also gives the client the opportunity to off-load their concerns, which helps them relax more easily.

Usually after 15-30 minutes, I have gathered all the information I need. Once the client appears comfortable, I ask them to move over to the recliner, and I then begin the hypnosis session. After the session, I ask if they feel disconnected from the problems they described prior to hypnosis. The answer is consistently positive. Then I ask them if the problems are anywhere in the room, and 75% say no.

Although clients can recall the pre-session conversation, after the hypnosis session, they feel separated from the problem. The over-whelming majority of first visit clients leave with a new, positive perspective regarding the concerns that brought them to my office. If they never follow up with another session, that new perspective fades away, and they revert back to the problem patterns. They must practice on a regular basis long enough to allow their feelings of empowerment to change from concept to lasting reality. They are establishing new patterns of thought that will lead to new behaviors.

IS HYPNOSIS THE SAME AS MEDITATION?

We all carry around repressed issues and emotions from our day-to-day lives. Over time, this accumulation leads to chronic emotional or physical problems. Too many people tend to ignore these problems, or pursue relief from them in the form of drugs, food, and/or alcohol. As an alternative, I recommend a consistent meditative/hypnosis practice as a way to create a foundation of inner peacefulness. Such a practice can enhance the overall quality of life, making one feel resilient even in the face of obstacles and difficulties.

When I meet with a client for the first time, I ask if they have ever practiced any form of meditation or relaxation techniques. If they have, I explain the similarity between what they already know and hypnosis, which helps them more easily enter the flow of hypnosis.

I think of hypnosis as meditation with intention. The word meditation comes from two Latin words: *meditari*, which means "to exercise the mind, or to think or dwell upon." *Mederi* means "to heal." Meditation is the process of focusing within, quieting the "static" of daily concerns, and creating a moment of inner stillness. Clients often express frustration with meditation because they either weren't given an adequate explanation of how to do it, or weren't able to achieve the level of calm they desired. Through the course of our work together, clients learn how to do self-hypnosis, which helps them become more proficient with their meditative process.

My goal is for all of my clients to become self-practitioners. By learning how to independently access the feel-good state of hypnosis, they enhance the effectiveness of our formal sessions, which results in more lasting success overall. We are all hard-wired with the ability to focus within. With a little practice, this thoughtful journey can be a life-changing experience.

HOW CAN HYPNOSIS HELP?

Most people primarily think of hypnosis as a solution for smoking or excess weight. Those are certainly two of its most common applications, but there are literally hundreds more. For example, hypnosis can positively enhance how effectively the body works. Although I often use hypnosis to address weight and smoking problems, I also specialize in Irritable Bowel Syndrome (IBS) hypnosis. Hypnosis can significantly relieve IBS symptoms that many individuals struggle with for years. Hypnosis greatly reduces stress and discomfort while optimizing gastrointestinal motility.

Another unique way hypnosis can directly influence the body is by healing warts. Hypnosis enhances the immune system and redirects blood circulation, minimizing the flow of oxygen and nutrients to where the warts are located, making them dry up and disappear.

Hypnosis can also enhance athletic ability, sales, academic, and musical performance. It can facilitate the birthing process, decrease or eliminate difficulties with stress, anger, and fear, and can alter the perception and anticipation of pain.

We all follow the path of our most dominant thoughts. Hypnosis helps us to powerfully choose our thoughts and reshape our world. For example, if as children we were repeatedly exposed to certain unhealthy views about smoking, food choices, or sedentary living, and modeled our behavior on those beliefs, we would develop habits that made us prone to obesity or poor health.

Once patterns become part of our daily routine, they develop roots in the long-term memory or subconscious. If we repeat anything for 21-30 consecutive days, it becomes automatic or second nature to us. This is true for all our usual activities, such as how we perform during sports activities, memorizing material for exams, or how we approach our jobs.

Here is a great example of what I mean: as a hospice nurse, I routinely had a very difficult time talking with patients and their families about end-of-life transition. When I first started in hospice, I usually struggled to find the right words. Then one day, I noticed the words began to flow much more easily.

I remember one particular situation in which many family members had traveled from another state because the condition of their loved one was rapidly declining. When I arrived at the patient's home, 25 worried family members greeted me. To my surprise, I was calm and relaxed, and easily expressed my assessment of the situation. Thanks to simple repetition, I no longer felt awkward and tongue-tied dealing with highly emotional circumstances. After two years on the job, I had repeated the hospice process enough to be able to effectively perform my job, even in front of such a distressed and anxious family.

Repetition RULES for problems and solutions alike. Most of my hypnosis clients have been repeating unhealthy patterns for decades. They come to me feeling powerless and frustrated. Intellectually, they certainly know what the problem is and what they want to do about it, but over time their patterns have become so deeply rooted, change seems impossible.

Hypnosis is an extremely effective "change agent." I frequently describe how hypnosis establishes a direct connection between the client's current position and where they want to be. Once the connection is made, past difficulties disappear, enabling one to productively move forward in life. Success always comes more quickly and is longer lasting with the aid of hypnosis.

During hypnosis, clients get a powerful sense of what their success will look and feel like before it actually arrives. Every time they listen to a session, they lock onto their goal with laser-beam precision. Then the subconscious begins to initiate the necessary inner changes that support their desired success.

The more comfortable the client is with the hypnotist, the more productively he or she manifests success. To that end, I work to form a relationship of trust and cooperation with each client. If the individual values my guidance, they will follow the flow of the session. This results in a deeper level of self-awareness for the client.

Many people wonder if hypnosis is right for them, or how long their hypnosis-enhanced success might last. I tell them the winning formula is pretty simple; all they need to do is to score positively in the following three categories:

1) *Receptivity:* must be open-minded, and willing to follow simple instructions.

2) *Motivation:* must have a genuine desire to establish positive change.

3) *Consistency:* must we willing to practice daily to create lasting success.

I start educating my clients the first time we speak together. I review the abbreviated ABC's of hypnosis, and send them a follow-up email with links to an audio introduction, specifics about their program of choice, and an intake form. They also receive a link to video clips of my television show, highlighting past client success, referring physicians, and other practitioners in the field.

WHAT WE CONCEIVE, WE ACHIEVE

Life is a long string of choices and how we imagine ourselves strongly influences the choices we make. The only limitations are those we self-impose. A phrase from the popular DVD The Secret sums it up perfectly; "thoughts become things." If our predominant thoughts are based on stress, frustration, and failure, then that is what we should expect to manifest in our lives. How we think and what we think shapes our world.

Hypnosis is a simple tool enabling you to powerfully harness your thoughts and thereby accomplish dramatic positive change. By constantly imagining what you want, how it is going to look, and the joy you will feel when you achieve it, you are programming your subconscious to initiate the inner changes that will support your goals.

I had a client who became fearful of driving. Over a period of three years, she drove less and less. She constantly focused on her irrational fears and began to see herself as not being able to drive, which is exactly what happened. Over time, she became increasingly adept at envisioning and feeling her fear. During our initial conversation, she went into explicit detail about her problem, even just talking about it made her more and more emotional.

During the hypnosis session, I guided her along an imaginary drive in the country, something she used to enjoy. Then I had her imagine that the drive led to her home in the city. During hypnosis, she was able to reconnect with what she used to enjoy about driving; the independence and control it gave her, as well as the pleasure of being able to drive to destinations she wished to visit.

At the conclusion of the session, she surprised herself by saying that the notion of driving home that day seemed fine to her. Intellectually, she remembered her problem, but for that moment, she had a new vision. She saw herself as a confident driver. In twenty minutes, she had re-framed her view of the situation and felt ready to drive again.

Most problems are the result of repeating unproductive thoughts. Like anything else, if we do it enough, it becomes easy and automatic. This is true whether we're talking about athletics, academics, auto repair, or fishing. We are creatures of habit. If we habitually anticipate positive situations and experiences, that's what we should expect to experience in our lives.

WHEN WILL I SEE RESULTS?

Lasting success with hypnosis is a process. If problem patterns are repeated for years, shouldn't we expect a period of repetition in order to erase them? The good news is that, with hypnosis, lasting positive change can be achieved in weeks, not years.

To better comprehend the hypnosis process, it is helpful to understand how the mind works in establishing life patterns, both good and bad. As we go through our daily lives, we initiate patterns that can last a lifetime. Most of these patterns involve core values and beliefs that determine our life choices, and who we are as individuals.

During our school years, we reinforce existing patterns learned as toddlers, plus develop new ones. We develop automatic patterns of communication, humor, loyalty, and affection. As we mature, these patterns may serve us well when we enter the work world, putting food on our tables and gas in our cars. Similarly, if we've developed unproductive patterns, we will struggle in our careers as we struggled in school.

A child learning to play baseball celebrates wildly when they first connect the bat with the ball. If they continue to practice, they will gradually be able to aim the ball where they want it to go and control how hard they hit it. The same child, learning to play the piano, will sit hour after hour repeating scales, to the point of not needing to look at the keys.

The habitual nature of life plays an enormous role in determining the quality of our lives. By routinely repeating unproductive patterns, we run the risk of enabling them to grow roots. Unfortunately, the subconscious mind can't tell the difference between good or bad, right or wrong. Think of the subconscious as a greenhouse, able to grow roses or poison ivy with equal success. It is the conscious mind's job to decide what is a toxic weed or a flower worth keeping.

Because we tend to follow the pattern of our most dominant thoughts, for better or worse, a wonderful aspect of hypnosis is that it enables us to choose better thoughts. With positive repetition, one can establish patterns that support one's goals. Why reinvent the wheel; if repetition worked to create the problem, why not use the same approach to achieve a solution? All my clients receive a CD recording of each session, and by routinely listening to these recordings, they can easily take back control of their lives.

WHAT IF I DON'T WAKE UP?

"Waking up" is not a problem. Hypnosis is more an essential aspect of human nature than it is something you receive from others. In fact, one of the most commonly used phrases in the field is "all hypnosis is self-hypnosis." The hypnotist is simply the tour guide, helping individuals step down to a deeper level of awareness for the purpose of establishing positive change. The only power a hypnotist has is the power to help a client access their own subconscious thoughts.

Recall a moment in your past when you were daydreaming. As relaxed and disconnected from the outer world as you may have been, you would have had no problem snapping to attention if the occasion required it. Let's suggest that one of those moments was a particularly deep daydream experience, perhaps comparable to the depth of a hypnosis session, but there was no one there to guide you out of it. What would happen? You would doze off and wake up the same way you always wake up from a comfortable nap.

Hypnosis is not a battle of wills. If a person trusts that he or she is receiving the help they need, they will likely have an easier and more productive experience. The clients are the ones who decide if they want to relax and how deeply relaxed they would like to become. When individuals learn how they can comfortably and easily flow into the soothing experience of hypnosis, they are often eager to repeat the experience simply because it feels good.

Learning to create your own hypnosis experience, by practicing outside the office setting, increases your ability to self-direct your emergence from a session. Prior to each in-office hypnosis session, my clients perform self-hypnosis for the purpose of optimizing their proficiency with the process. By training self-practitioners, I encourage synergy between office and home sessions. You can click on the "self-hypnosis intro" at www.BurlingtonHypnosis.com to learn how easy it is.

WILL I CLUCK LIKE A CHICKEN?

Among serious-minded hypnosis practitioners, there are two schools of thought regarding entertainment or stage hypnosis. One group chooses to distance themselves from it because it has caused so much confusion and slowed the advancement of clinical hypnosis. The other group believes that without stage hypnosis, the healing side of the field would not be where it is today. I support the second group's perspective.

It wasn't until the scientific community began to validate hypnosis's immensely positive health benefits that it truly began to shine. I consider stage hypnosis performers as first responders. For most of the 20th century, they performed CPR on this fragile technique, until it was strong enough to stand on its own. During the early days, any publicity was good publicity.

Stage hypnosis was legitimized by the late Ormond McGill (1913–2005), who was referred to as the Dean of American hypnotists. Mr. McGill pioneered hypnosis as a form of entertainment, and authored many books. His 1947 publication, The Encyclopedia of Genuine Stage Hypnotism, became known as the bible of stage hypnosis. I had the distinct advantage of seeing Mr. McGill perform at the National Guild of Hypnotists' annual convention in 2004. To see video clips of his work search 'Ormond McGill' at www.youtube.com.

There are four key components to stage hypnosis:

1) The volunteers are usually less inhibited an more open to what is asked of them.

2) Using a suggestibility test, the most hypnotizable volunteers are invited to participate.

3) Volunteers understand that the audience expects them to perform.

4) The hypnotist employs rapid induction or fast hypnotic technique.

During a performance, the hypnotist asks for volunteers. To select the most hypnotizable volunteers, the hypnotist does a suggestibility test. For example, the volunteers are asked to close their eyes and hold both arms out in front of them. Then they are directed to imagine that a bunch of large, helium-filled balloons are tied to their right wrist, and a 10-pound bucket of water is suspended from their left hand.

After simple relaxation instructions and hypnotic suggestion, some members of the audience begin lifting their right arm and dropping their left arm. These are the most suggestible volunteers, who are then invited to participate in the show. Once on stage, peer pressure kicks in. With a room full of people expecting them to do what they are instructed to do, the volunteers feel compelled to oblige.

The hypnotist then employs what is referred to as rapid induction or fast hypnosis. This technique quickly leads the volunteers into a deep hypnotic trance. At this point, the hypnotist makes humorous suggestions to the volunteers, asking them to perform actions that will entertain the audience. It is important to know that those who participate in hypnosis of any kind even in a stage setting, are always in control, and would never do anything against their will.

DOES INSURANCE COVER HYPNOSIS?

For the most part, health insurance does not cover the expense of hypnosis. Individuals should expect to be responsible for the full cost of their sessions. Some insurance companies do offer discounts to subscribers who see participating clinicians, however.

David Eisenberg, M.D. spearheaded a nationwide telephone survey of 1,539 randomly selected Americans over the age of 18. His study reported that 36% of the respondents said they have been to a Complementary Alternative Medicine (CAM) provider in 1990. This was significantly higher than previously reported. (*Journal of Alt.* and *Comp. Medicine.* Dec. 2001)

$10.3 billion was spent out-of-pocket on CAM related services, which equaled the 1990 out-of-pocket expenditures for hospitalizations. (*New England Journal of Medicine* in 1993)

BEDTIME STORY

With words, the hypnotist guides the client into a relaxed state. When the client reaches this deeper level of awareness, their subconscious mind becomes open and receptive. At the same time, the conscious mind, which normally acts as gatekeeper, takes a break.

The process of guiding individuals into hypnotic trance couldn't be easier. It is like reading a child a bedtime story. The story activates the child's imagination, which is located in the subconscious mind. As the story progresses, and the subconscious opens more and more, the child becomes totally immersed in the story, losing all awareness of physical self.

The process in the office is similar, but with a purpose. Once I have gathered all the client's pertinent information, reviewed how hypnosis works, and what they can expect to experience, we begin the actual hypnosis session. I make sure the client is comfortable, offer them a blanket, and have them remove glasses if they wear them. I have a very comfortable recliner in my office and I encourage the client to elevate their legs and tip their head back.

Then I give them a pair of headphones and turn on my lapel microphone and the background music. They close their eyes and the "bedtime story" begins. Most of my hypnosis sessions run about 20–25 minutes long and one third of each session is devoted to achieving deep hypnotic trance.

Here is an example of one of my favorite sessions:

You may begin by taking a few cleansing deep breaths and then just allow yourself this momentary luxury of relaxation. Focus on these words as you begin to easily initiate this inner shift to where relaxation becomes more and more apparent to you.

I give you full authority for these next few minutes to release your outer thoughts; set them aside for now, and consider the possibility that wonderfully soothing inner comfort is your reward. Now that you have accepted the general concept of relaxation, begin to experience it. Imagine that just because I suggest that relaxation might occur, and also because you likely think it would be good if it did, it does.

So now imagine that you can step down into relaxation and experience it as it grows and spreads. Take this unique opportunity to just drift along, listening, but not listening, asleep but not asleep at all. Perhaps your conscious mind expects to experience a certain level of comfort and your subconscious expects something much deeper than that.

As you start to release and relax more and more, perhaps you might think about or imagine that you are lounging under a gazebo next to a country river, on a perfect summer day. Imagine you comfortably lying there with nothing to do, and nowhere to go, listening to the comforting flowing sounds of the river and relaxing more deeply, more peacefully with every cleansing breath you take.

With a gentle summer breeze whispering in your ear, you choose to release and allow the river sounds to carry you down to wonderful new depths of inner comfort and serenity. Just allow and direct the steady flow of the river to automatically carry away any leftover unproductive thoughts, worries, stress, or concerns. Imagine they are all quickly released with each breath out.

Imagine that the river carries them away, leaving you safely and comfortably able to melt down even more deeply and completely. This is your time, right here, right now, to embrace this inner stillness; allow it to flow and saturate you. You are feeling free and ready to release and relax, feeling totally at peace now. Anything and everything that would have prevented such a deep enjoyable experience is floating away, down the river, enabling you to go even more deeply into relaxation.

You are just lying there, allowing the river to work its peaceful magic, just enjoying and relaxing, releasing and immersing yourself down into this inner sanctuary of comfort. You have complete control and may become as relaxed and peaceful as you choose. The comforting swirling water soothes you and carries you more deeply, as your thoughts float and drift, and your body absolutely melts beneath you.

As you begin to really enjoy this inner journey, imagine a gentle sun shower passes by. A summer afternoon of pure relaxing rain surrounds the gazebo. With hypnosis we direct this soothing afternoon rain shower to affect you in a wonderfully relaxing way. Imagine that this is special rain. Imagine that it is here to calm and relax you even more than before.

With the rain comes the scent of purity in the air. Imagine the rain purifies the air around you, instantly allowing and directing you to release any remaining fragments of stress, worry, or concern. The sounds of the rain hitting the leaves and of the river flowing along are so relaxing that you release and let go even more.

Notice that you now begin to inhale this purified air surrounding you, and it gently carries you down to a deeper, more peaceful level of serenity. Your senses are now completely surrounded and saturated with the sound of the steady flow of the country river, the gentle tapping of an afternoon rain, and the relaxing purity of the air you breathe.

Allow yourself to become a part of all of nature's splendor as it surrounds, comforts, and soothes you. As you continue to peacefully breathe and relax, notice how your thoughts drift in and out, as though they were drops of water in the river.

Imagine your thoughts as droplets in the river as you become aware of how the water collects in a large pool. Imagine that the pool is still and very deep. No movement at all except for the slight ripple caused by a fallen leaf. Your thoughts flow very much like this river. At times they are quick and fleeting, and other times, like now, they are slow, steady, and very, very deep. Open yourself to experience new levels of peaceful comfort, self-awareness, and freedom.

WEIGHT LOSS HYPNOSIS

The entire June 2004 issue of Time magazine was devoted to the subject of obesity. One study reported that the children of today believe that fast food is healthier than home-cooked meals and another stated that today's youth is predicted to have a shorter life expectancy than that of their parents for the first time in American history. (Stanford Prevention Research Center 2007)

Another study reported medical spending, due to obesity, to be as much as $92.6 billion in 2002 dollars, or 9% of U.S. health expenditures. (Finkelstein EA 2003) Another study reported how, in the last 30 years, obesity has dramatically increased for adults and children. The prevalence of obesity in adults 20 to 74 years of age from 1976–1980 increased from 15% to 33% in the 2003–2004 survey. (cdc.gov)

I conduct more weight-loss hypnosis sessions than any other course of treatment. Obesity-related patterns like poor nutrition, sedentary living, and emotional eating become problematic with repetition. Over time, unhealthy patterns become rooted in the subconscious mind. As a result, individuals feel powerless to change. Like a computer hard drive, the subconscious stores whatever information it is given.

Unfortunately, the traditional response to obesity is dieting, which is a conscious-level solution to a subconscious-level problem. The multibillion-dollar dieting industry focuses on the pounds rather than on the pattern. An analogy would be if a physician only treated the cough, rather than prescribing antibiotics for the infection that caused the cough.

My approach with weight-challenged clients is to help them change their goal from losing weight to living well. During hypnosis, the subconscious can be directed in two positive ways: to release unhealthy patterns and to begin focusing on the life the client prefers. When clients release unproductive patterns from the past, they begin to see and feel a new, healthier, fitter version of themselves.

Hypnosis melts away the struggle, making it easier to move forward. My clients use hypnosis to create a linear connection between where they are now and where they want to go in life. With all the frustration and failure removed from the equation, thoughts and images of fitness success begin to take shape. By routinely repeating this process, individuals train their brain to initiate the necessary inner changes to succeed.

By routinely listening to home reinforcement CDs, individuals become proficient at imagining what their ultimate goal means to them. These powerful images then influence their actions, supporting new positive values and beliefs. If your brain realizes that your overall goal is to live well, then the weight takes care of itself.

I also ask clients to limit weighing themselves to once a month. We live in an extremely polarized, pass/fail society. Frequent weigh-ins can result in disappointment because of unrealistic expectations as to how much and how quickly weight loss should occur. By focusing more on how they feel about their plan, and how loosely their clothes begin to fit, their focus shifts from the struggle of weight loss to long-term success.

DONNA'S WEIGHT LOSS STORY

Donna (not her real name) was in her late 40s, and was looking for help with weight loss. She was significantly overweight and described her biggest weakness as unrelenting emotional eating during the evening hours. She was also in the middle of a nasty divorce, had three teenage children, and a demanding job.

She had seen an episode of my television program featuring a weight-loss client. She was fascinated, not so much by the client's 40-pound weight loss, but by his description of how hypnosis made him feel more centered and grounded than he had ever felt before.

The reason I am sharing Donna's experience is because it is an excellent example of being asked to treat the symptom rather than the cause. It was pretty evident during Donna's first visit that obesity was not her primary problem. She had been badly treated throughout 22 years of marriage, and described how cruelly her husband conducted himself throughout the divorce proceedings.

Donna confessed that she couldn't remember her last moment of inner peace and that she also suffered from chronic insomnia. Having been brought up in a home that used food for emotional relief and celebration, she resorted to what she knew best. Every night she ate uncontrollably.

Unfortunately Donna had married the wrong man. He physically and emotionally abused her throughout their marriage, and treated her like an enemy rather than the mother of their children. She simply didn't know what to do, so she did the only thing that made her feel good, which was to eat.

After I had assessed where Donna's difficulties truly lay, I started to describe the process of hypnosis. I explained how she would be guided to become peacefully disconnected from all of her issues, so that she could begin to take control of her life. At the time, her stress level was so high that she doubted that she could even be hypnotized at all.

I told her that it was my experience that clients overwhelmed with anxiety usually do well with hypnosis. Even though the concept of deep, relaxing comfort seems so foreign to them, it is, in fact, exactly what they need, and for this reason, they usually have no problem getting into the flow.

Due to Donna's situation, I knew she needed more than a traditional approach supporting proper nutrition, exercise, and motivation. Instead, we focused on severing the emotional connection to her husband and the divorce proceedings. During the hypnosis sessions, she was guided to accept the notion of being in his presence in body but not in spirit. Using imagery, she was able to rehearse how she wanted to look and feel every time she had to be around her husband, especially in court.

Donna surprised herself with the depth of relaxation she achieved in her first session. She tearfully described how peaceful and happy she felt. During that session, she experienced complete separation from her emotional burdens. Not only do clients often experience profound freedom through hypnosis, but usually the accumulated distress of the past seems to dissolve naturally. I explained to Donna that listening to her CD sessions at home would increase the distance between her and her problems. Two weeks later she came back for her second visit. The difference was remarkable. She was relaxed and happy.

Once Donna had a way to regain her personal power, everything changed for the better. Subsequent sessions included more traditional weight-loss strategies, and she absolutely took control.

She started to feel good about herself, the weight melted away, and she was able to envision the new and improved version of herself. Positive change starts with a thought, which evolves into positive action, which leads to a positive new approach to life.

To me, the most exciting aspect of hypnosis is how anyone can do it anytime they choose. We all have the ability to focus our thoughts and create dramatic change in our lives. With just a little practice, what once seemed impossible is achieved, and when one realizes that he or she is the one affecting such a change, success continues.

WEIGHT-LOSS HYPNOSIS SESSION

A weight-loss hypnosis session begins with relaxing the client. Once the client is guided into a comfortably deep hypnotic trance, the therapeutic portion of the session begins. This involves simple directions supporting the individual's goals and desires. It is important to present new suggestions and imagery in such a way that the client can embrace them and begin to act upon them.

Here is an example of a weight-loss session I frequently use:

Your subconscious mind is now open, active, and ready to download positive new applications, directing you towards a lifetime of fitness fulfillment. With hypnosis you choose to make the absolute healthy choice to change from within. The old way has led you to where you are today, but you are through with it now, and choose to release it once and for all.

So your new journey of inner power and freedom of choice begins here and now. From now on, you choose to focus on your fitness success each time you relax with hypnosis. Your thoughts are positive, life-affirming, and hypnotically optimized to create and support the level of fitness you know you can achieve, because it is what you want for yourself now, and you will not settle for anything less than healthy fitness success.

Your subconscious is directed with hypnosis to create and enhance new motivation and enthusiasm to continue along this exciting new path of consistent healthy living. Hypnosis creates a wonderful new mindfulness; it connects you to your own inner truth, beyond the excuses, alibis, and rationalizations. It liberates you from a world of procrastination, self-doubt, and hopelessness.

The first change you make with hypnosis is your relationship with food. You will be creating and embracing a relaxed, enjoyable mealtime. Most people that want to lose weight think that they need to starve themselves or deny themselves the foods they enjoy. That self-defeating mentality stops today.

Thousands of years of evolution have trained our bodies to respond in crisis whenever we go without food or there is not enough food. Dieting triggers the survival mode in all of us; sure you may reach a temporary plateau, but the body fights back, and you eventually put all the weight back on.

Your new plan supporting lasting, fitness success has four simple rules.

> *Rule #1* states that when you are hungry you will eat. This is very important; your body needs fuel, and it will let you know when it is running low. By responding to your body's call for nutrition, your metabolism is optimized and productive, making it easier for you to become free of excess weight. So it's okay to eat, and eating healthfully is even better.

> *Rule #2* states that you should eat what you enjoy eating. Traditional dieting involves eating foods you don't enjoy, which ensures failure sooner or later. Ask one of your thin friends if they sacrifice enjoyable nutrition to maintain their level of fitness; more than likely they don't.

By eating what you like, you aren't begrudging yourself what you want, which eliminates the ongoing negative conflicts involved with dieting.

Rule #3 states that when you eat, you do so consciously, focused on the meal and nothing else; which means no television, texting, or telephones. When one eats consciously, they have the opportunity to savor the meal, which heightens the experience. You will also eat slowly, chewing each mouthful 20 times and placing knife and fork on the table as you do. This mindful approach helps you to become more aware of healthy choices and the success you pursue.

Rule #4 states that when you are comfortable—not full— you will stop eating. It doesn't matter what is left on the plate. Your new priority is to only fuel your body with what it needs to be healthy, fit, and strong. When you are comfortable, the meal is concluded. Hundreds of calories can be avoided if you stop when you are comfortable, as opposed to when you are full.

Your goal is not to simply lose weight, but rather to live well. With this expanded focus, and the four simple rules, the weight takes care of itself. No doubt, you have wanted to make this change for some time now. Perhaps you have tried many times before, but haven't had success or maybe your success was short lived. So now you're choosing to go deeper with hypnosis, down to the level that assures that everything you accept comes to be, easily and naturally.

Until now, permanent change regarding your healthy fitness has been elusive. The reason is simple repetition. In the past, whenever you ate unhealthfully, or embraced sedentary living, you reinforced those patterns. Over time, with repetition, they became deeply rooted in your long-term memory or subconscious mind.

The good news is that with hypnosis you have unique access to your inner storage facility, as we now begin the process of uninstalling and deleting the outdated junk from your past, and installing new applications, assuring long-term fitness success.

Because it is your wish to become healthy and fit and because you are now free and able to make this choice, you now chose to do just that. Because living an active, fit, healthy life is something you truly value, and realizing now that you have the power to choose; you are now choosing to become the healthy, fit person of your dreams.

You have decided to start fresh, to choose the life you want rather than settling for second best. And because you truly are free to make this choice, to live a fit, healthy life, to become active and thrive, so it shall be. The old way is over; done, finished, finally and forever. The heavy, sedentary part of you is gone now; you have released it and you feel so ready to thrive.

You are now so open and receptive to empowering healthy change that your dynamic subconscious mind is accepting and integrating all of this new information in such a positive way, your success is a foregone conclusion; it's automatic.

To you, right now, the old way is done; it is over, finished, finally and forever. You have made a powerful choice to change. Whatever has been holding you back has been released, and each time you relax in this way, you train your brain to continue to support this new life plan of improved energy, self-image, confidence, and fitness success.

By routinely relaxing in this way, you deeply prepare your mind and body for absolute fitness success. You develop a plan, make lists of healthy foods you actually enjoy, explore enjoyable ways to become active and happy, and you drink an ideal amount of pure, refreshing water every day. Already you feel good; already you feel free. You feel as though you have an inner plan, down deep, which is transforming what once seemed difficult into something easy, enjoyable, productive, and exciting. During this process you will never feel as though you are denying yourself anything, ever.

Right now you are looking forward to moving forward. You feel more in control than ever before. You know who you are, and are now choosing where you want to go in life, how you want to look and feel, and you understand that healthy positive change is yours for the taking, starting right now, and it feels fantastic.

More and more, you are becoming an unstoppable force on a non-stop mission to fitness success. Your positive awareness is growing; you are now becoming more mindful of all the simple changes that lead you to long-lasting fitness success.

SMOKING CESSATION

I love helping clients sever their smoking connection. They come in hopelessly desperate for help and leave with newfound confidence that they can easily move forward, smoke-free.

I once treated a 72-year-old truck driver, Joe, who smoked three packs a day for 30 years. He was so desperate and worried about his health, he would do absolutely anything to be free. In a tearful discussion, he shared his fear of not seeing his grandchildren grow up.

After the first two hypnosis sessions, he was giddy with hope. Joe came back a week later for his third session. He walked into the office grinning from ear to ear. "I have not touched a smoke all week," he told me. We did his third session and I sent him on his way. Six months later I got a note from Joe saying he was still smoke-free. He included a heartfelt letter from his eight-year-old granddaughter, thanking me for "saving her Grandpa's life."

One reason smokers do so consistently well with hypnosis is because they are fearful for their health and wellbeing, which translates into high levels of motivation. Motivated individuals with nowhere else to turn are my favorite clients.

It is all about repetition. If a smoker takes 20 puffs per cigarette and smokes a pack per day, he or she is repeating the problem pattern 400 times a day and 146,000 times a year. Think of the possibilities if you applied that level of consistent repetition to a life-affirming activity instead.

Most clients are unaware that the seeds of the smoking pattern are sown very early in life. The first time a four-year-old child sees a parent smoke a cigarette, the acceptance of smoking may begin to take root. Every time that child sees someone smoke, the motivation to smoke grows, until one day it transforms from a thought into an action.

The first cigarette is an interesting experience; just because the thought of smoking has been nurtured and cultivated for years does not mean the body necessarily agrees with the plan. I recall my first cigarette and my reaction was typical; I gagged and choked my way through the entire cigarette. If most first-time smokers have such an unpleasant experience, why would they ever go back for more?

Suppose you went into a new restaurant and ordered a meal you had never had before, but anticipated a great dining experience. The meal arrived and looked delicious, but your first taste repulsed you in every way. It tasted so vile it made you physically ill. As a result, it is safe to assume that you would likely never order that dish again and probably never go to that restaurant again.

If the response to both situations is similar, why would the diner stay clear of the meal, but the smoker continue to smoke? The answer is that smoking was programmed and reinforced years before the event. There was no such reinforcement in the case of the culinary catastrophe.

Unfortunately, enough first-time smokers continue the habit to support a multibillion-dollar industry responsible for killing 5.4 million people per year worldwide and predicted to annually kill 6.5 million people by the year 2015. (World Health Organization)

When smokers attempt to use conscious means to quit, they usually encounter withdrawal in the form of cravings, mood swings, or even weight gain. Withdrawal is conflict between the conscious and subconscious mind. Consciously, you want to stop smoking, but your subconscious protests, demanding what the "program" calls for.

Hypnosis is a way of communicating with the subconscious, helping it to understand and accept the new, healthier pattern. By routinely reinforcing the solution, it grows roots of its own and quickly becomes the pattern of choice, conflict-free.

I see smokers for two office visits. During the initial visit, they learn self-hypnosis and receive two stop-smoking hypnosis sessions. They return within a week and receive a third session. They go home with a CD recording of the three sessions and are instructed to listen once a day. The formula is simple; repetition created the problem, so we use the same approach for the solution. Because hypnosis formally opens the vault and pile-drives the preferred message deeply into the subconscious mind, lasting positive change can come easily.

In one study, patients received individualized hypnosis for smoking cessation over three sessions. 81% reported they stopped smoking completely and 48% reported abstinence for at least 12 months post-treatment. 95% of patients were satisfied with the treatment they received. (*Int. Jnl. of Clin. and Exp. Hyp.* 2004)

RON'S SMOKE-FREE SUCCESS STORY

Debby was desperate to get her husband, Ron (not their real names), off of cigarettes. He was 44 years old and becoming less active and more short of breath. To make matters worse, Ron worked from home, so he had the freedom to smoke all day. He wanted to quit and had tried all the patches and gum without success. When Debby brought up the idea of hypnosis, Ron initially balked at the idea.

Ron is like many clients I see. He used to think hypnosis was more a parlor trick than a legitimate way to establish positive change. What changed his mind was the growing number of people he knew who succeeded with hypnosis.

Ron confided that his father died of lung cancer. He tried to hide his worries from Debby, but he knew he wasn't fooling anyone. When I explained how hypnosis was like a daydream-on-demand, and that he would feel more relaxed than he had ever been, he was eager to give it a try.

Once the myths and misconceptions are dispelled, the rest is pretty easy. Because of Ron's strong desire to quit, and his concern for his health, he connected quickly to the therapeutic message of each of the sessions. After the first session, he felt new hope about his chances for success. Intellectually, he remembered his past failures at quitting, but after hypnosis he described feeling a powerful confidence he had never previously experienced.

When Debby came to pick up Ron, she immediately saw a change. He was calm, and described his confidence in feeling as though his smoking days were now behind him. When he came back for his second office visit two weeks later, he was smiling and smoke-free. His final hypnosis session was much deeper and even more meaningful than the previous sessions, which is usually the case with nearly all of my clients.

It's the feel-good aspect of hypnosis that excites people to learn more, to release, and to let go. They begin to believe in their ability to create the life they want with their thoughts. It all snowballs into an empowering flow of positive energy, making it nearly impossible to fail.

Six months after I see each client, I send them a satisfaction survey to make sure I am on track and doing a good job. Ron's survey came back with a small gold star neatly placed next to each of the survey questions. He also wrote an additional note at the bottom, saying that he had lost 20 pounds as he was now running again. Ron was a track star in college and was thrilled when his inner athlete reemerged. Through hypnosis, he was able to release a negative pattern and reconnect with a positive one.

SMOKING CESSATION HYPNOSIS SESSION

Every smoker fears what's to come if they continue to smoke. Some verbalize their fears, while others prefer to ignore or repress them. I'm not a big fan of aversion therapy, or scaring individuals with stark scenarios detailing smoking-related illnesses. I prefer to create a framework and then allow the client, in the privacy of their thoughts, to fill in the blanks.

A hypnosis approach called future- pace technique guides the client into a future moment in which they can create positive, vivid images and emotions. One of my hypnosis programs gives the client the unique opportunity to not only understand their darkest fears about the future, but to also make the better choice. Here is an example of what I mean:

As you relax so deeply and release so completely, imagine you are walking down a country road on a perfect sunny day. You can clearly see the beauty of nature around you as you continue along until you come to a fork in the road. The road to the right leads you into your smoke-free future. You will get to see and feel the freedom and relief that awaits you.

To truly appreciate this healthy decision of a lifetime, it could be helpful to visit what might have been. That's right; the road to the left leads you into what would have been your smoking future. Imagine that you now move quickly into your smoking future. Imagine you quickly move forward one year from today.

In this image, you are continuing to smoke, perhaps even more than you do now. Now move forward five years from today; see how you have aged and the worry and concern in your eyes as you puff away, imprisoned by the unfortunate choice you made so long ago.

Now move forward in time, 10 years from today. See and feel the toll smoking has taken. You are weaker now; still smoking though. Go forward to the time when perhaps illness awaits. See and feel yourself physically and emotionally compromised because of smoking; you are dependent on others for care, surrounded by family and loved ones.

As you lie there, you can only think about the healthy choice you never made; you are experiencing deep feelings of sadness and regret. Take from this all you need to truly understand the healthy life you wish to have. Take from these words and images all you need to ensure the positive, healthy choice you are about to make.

Now return to the present time. Remaining deeply relaxed, come back to 10 years into your smoking future, then five years, then one year into your smoking future, and finally imagine you are back at the fork in the road, with a new focus and determination to succeed. Now experience a positive burst of exhilarating energy as you quickly proceed along the road to the right, your future smoke-free success. See and feel yourself one year from today, completely smoke-free in every way. You freed yourself with hypnosis and never looked back, experiencing no cravings, withdrawal, or problem of any kind.

Move forward five years into your future, smoke-free success; you are feeling and looking fantastic in every way. You have more energy; you are healthy and happy in every way. See and feel the resilient smile of healthy confidence telling you that you will be smoke-free for life, and it feels so good.

Go forward now; imagine 10 years into your future, smoke-free success. From this point in your future, smoke-free success, look back to the moment that you knew success was yours. Perhaps it was when you learned about hypnosis, and took control for good. Allow this moment of clarity to grow and spread within you.

Every, word, thought, and any extra sounds reinforce your comfort, relaxation, and smoke-free success. As you go through your daily life, every time you hear a telephone ring, you will be reminded, redirected, and reconnected to your smoke-free success.

The part of you connected in any way to your smoking past is becoming weak, powerless, and frail. The part of you determined to take control of your healthy wellbeing is doing just that. The healthy part of you is rapidly becoming stronger, more resourceful, and forever committed to this new life plan.

You are now supercharged with all the knowledge, skill, and determination you will ever need to succeed. From now on, everything becomes easier and more natural. Everything positive about you grows, saturating and spreading within you.

You clearly understand now that smoking never added anything positive to your life or helped you in any way. At one time, maybe when you were very young, smoking may have represented maturity or perhaps you simply smoked because you saw others do so. That was when you were young and unable to make the right choice.

Those days are gone. You are an adult now, and capable of deciding what you want and what you don't want in your life. From now on, today and every day, you value healthy living first and foremost. Smoking is gone from your thoughts and actions forever. Gone is the expense, and the foul-smelling breath and clothing. Gone is the shortness of breath and all the worry about illness and a shorter life. A new cycle of healthy freedom has arrived and it just feels right to you.

The more you reinforce these words, and create the images they imply, the more deeply rooted they become in shaping your smoke-free success. These powerful words and images take positive effect immediately. The more frequently you listen to this session or sessions like it, the easier it is for you to take total control for life.

You will truly enjoy this smoke-free transition and from it only wonderfully healthy and beneficial changes come into your life; some in subtle unassuming ways and others in an unexpected and spectacular fashion.

STRESS RELIEF

One of my recent stress clients spent the first 20 minutes of her first session emotionally detailing every issue related to her stress. I waited to speak until she seemed finished, and then I waited a while longer. She had no experience with hypnosis, but was so desperate; she was determined to make it work.

After her first-ever hypnosis experience, I asked her if she still felt the weight of the stress, to which she emotionally answered "no." I then asked her if any of the past stress, worry, or concerns were anywhere in the room and she said "no." Then I asked her if she felt confident about moving forward, using hypnosis to ensure this comfort would last and she said, with a big smile, "most definitely."

There is no other holistic or mainstream medical intervention that can create such a dramatic, rapid disconnect from the unwanted, unhealthy patterns of the past. In addition to such instant freedom, stressed clients bask so deeply in the calming glow of hypnosis because it is the opposite of how they usually feel.

Time magazine's June 6, 1983 cover story called stress "The Epidemic of the Eighties," and referred to it as our leading health problem. A 1996 Prevention magazine survey reported that 75% of the population feels they experience "great stress" one day a week, with one out of three indicating they feel this way more than twice a week. It is estimated that 75 to 90% of all visits to primary care physicians are for stress-related problems. (Stress.org)

43% percent of adults suffer adverse health effects from stress; 67% of family physician office visits are due to stress-related symptoms; 64% of Americans say they are taking steps to reduce stress in their lives. Stress is linked to the leading causes of death: heart disease, cancer, lung ailments, accidents, cirrhosis of the liver, and suicide. (APA 2005)

During the last 25 years, the world has changed dramatically, and our ability to cope with it in a healthy way is being challenged more than ever before. We feel little control over what's happening in our lives—whether it's unemployment, the economy, threats to the environment, or concerns about our general safety. Technology keeps us plugged into each other and to the media, which increases ratings by keeping us shocked and scared.

As a result, I see a steady stream of stressed-out clients who have lost their sense of self and life purpose. They usually have an extremely polarized view of the world, which leaves no margin for error; they are either 100% right or 100% wrong about everything they do. As a result they feel trapped, and the harder they try to meet unrealistic standards, the worse they feel about themselves and the more stressed they become. Left unchecked, stress causes feelings of uncomfortable annoyance, then physical and or emotional symptoms, and eventually illness.

One healthy way to relieve symptoms of stress is through exercise. Although this is a great way to burn off nervous energy, it does nothing to relieve the underlying problem. The uncomfortable feelings of stress are actually a symptom, the same way excess weight is the symptom of obesity, it is not the problem. The source of stress is how we view and respond to the world around us. Unfortunately, self-medication in the form of alcohol, drugs, or food is usually our first line of defense. This approach may feel good for a while, but does not get to the source of the problem and often leads to other problems.

To make matters worse, we are our own worse critics, and chronic, negative self-talk results in unfulfilled expectations that snowball into ongoing stress. What we think about, we bring about. If I were fearful of driving and routinely reminded myself of how uncomfortable I felt driving on the highway, and each time focused on how bad it was, I would run the risk of creating habitual driving stress.

How we respond to people and situations is not an accident. The good news is that we all have the natural ability to replace what doesn't work with something that does. That is why hypnosis is so helpful in reshaping one's life view. One of the significant benefits of my stress-relief hypnosis program is that my clients know that it's working after their very first session. The calming tranquility they experience is such a welcome oasis from what they are used to that they bond very quickly to the process, and experience an immediate positive shift.

Underneath the immediate feel-good aspect of hypnosis lies the therapeutic portion of each session, which is designed to systematically unplug, delete, and un-install connections to values and beliefs that create stress. With the help of creative suggestions, positive imagery, and metaphors, clients are able to establish change from within.

The previously mentioned future-pace technique helps the individual to shape images of success. For example, a client with fear of flying can create a vision of enjoying a comfortable plane ride. The vision can seem so real that they may experience tears of joy at the conclusion of the session. One reason hypnosis is such a unique option is that it is a point-of-source treatment. Rather than offering temporary comfort like a great massage, it locates and unplugs the source of the problem, and with repetition, the solution sticks.

CHERYL'S STRESS-RELIEF SUCCESS

Cheryl was raised in a home with an alcoholic father who constantly wreaked emotional and physical havoc on her and her siblings. By the time she was eight years old, her mother decided she and her children had endured enough and hustled them out of the house in the middle of the night, and sought refuge with relatives in a nearby state.

Because of her turbulent childhood, Cheryl developed unhealthy, stressful reactions to the world around her. Over time, she became conditioned to experience symptoms of stress whenever she was in the presence of her father or any authority figure.

Cheryl described herself as always being on edge. She was a constant worrier, whose predominant thoughts focused on fear, powerlessness, and negativity. On her first visit, I did a lot of listening. Active listening helps to develop rapport with clients, especially those who have trust issues.

When I described the relief she might experience during a hypnosis session, Cheryl was very skeptical. She had been in crisis mode for so long, it was all she knew. Once the hypnosis session began, Cheryl, like many overly stressed individuals, slid very quickly and deeply into hypnotic trance. During the session, I guided her to a creative level of thought where she could easily imagine empowering scenarios of her future.

I suggested she might imagine herself at home preparing to watch a DVD. When she pressed play, she would see a movie of her future self. I asked her to carry the deep comfort and peace that she was experiencing from hypnosis into the image of her future life. In the image, she was guided to see and feel the positive changes that could result.

Prior to the session, Cheryl mentioned several situations and people she routinely had difficulty with. During hypnosis, she was able to replay those scenarios, but this time with a different outcome. In her fantasy image, she was focused, in control, and centered. She was also more connected to rational thought, and able to release the events of the distant past, freeing herself to move forward in life with confidence.

After the session, Cheryl was emotional and said she felt as if her perspective had shifted. She described how her fears and worries had become distant and vague. Intellectually or consciously, she remembered how things used to be, but now she felt free of the grip of her negative past.

On her first visit, Cheryl talked nonstop about her father, the abuse and all the negative energy of her past. When she returned for visit two, she was a different person; she was smiling and light-hearted. In just two weeks, her mood, and more importantly her perspective, had dramatically changed for the better. She was totally focused on her future. She decided to go back to school and she also broke up with her boyfriend. She also mentioned the many positive comments she had received from friends and coworkers about her positive attitude shift.

Hypnosis is the ultimate reframing tool. It can help individuals to instantly feel completely differently about people, habits, or situations. Once this positive shift is accomplished, routine home reinforcement sessions lock the positive change in place, ensuring lasting freedom from troubling issues.

IRRITABLE BOWEL SYNDROME

As a registered nurse, I have always leaned toward the medical side of hypnosis. I feel especially qualified to help individuals with chronic anxiety, stress, and pain, which is why I chose to specialize in irritable bowel syndrome (IBS) hypnosis. IBS is a chronic gastro-intestinal condition (GI) with no known cause or cure. Symptoms include any one, or a combination of the following: diarrhea, constipation, cramping, gas, pain, nausea, vomiting, or bloating. Symptoms usually run in cycles, lasting for days, months, or years. Many IBS sufferers feel like prisoners in their own home.

IBS affects 35 million Americans, 4 out of 5 of which are women. It is more prevalent than asthma, diabetes, acid reflux, and depression combined. There are likely millions of IBS sufferers who never pursue treatment due to embarrassment. 10% of all primary care physician visits are IBS-related. It is the second leading cause for employee absenteeism, and costs the U.S. 8 billion dollars a year.

Diagnosing IBS is a process of exclusion, which means a physician needs to initially rule out conditions such as lactose intolerance, Crohn's disease, bacterial infections, parasites, dumping syndrome, ulcerative colitis, inflammatory bowel disease, celiac disease, and gallbladder disease before a diagnosis of IBS can be determined.

Many confuse inflammatory bowel disease (IBD) with IBS. There are 2 types of IBD; Crohn's disease and ulcerative colitis. The abnormalities caused by either will show up in x-rays, which is not the case with IBS.

The onset of IBS symptoms usually occurs between the ages of 20-29 in adults and ages 9-11 in children. IBS can sometimes be traced back to a traumatic event, illness, injury, or accident. Some individuals, however, begin having symptoms for no apparent reason at all. IBS is also known to be familial, which means IBS can be passed down through generations.

Many IBS sufferers go through life with no idea of what normal GI function is like. Symptoms can also be aggravated by stress, chocolate, caffeine, alcohol, foods high in animal or vegetable fat, beverages containing dyes, artificial sweeteners, food or medication sensitivities, or hormone fluctuation. Although these factors can play a role in the disease, none are the cause.

Traditional medical intervention includes high-fiber diets, anti-spasmodics to relieve cramping and spasms, antidepressants to relieve the emotional impact, and anti-diarrhea medication. Research indicates the aforementioned is only 25% effective. Because IBS is not life-threatening, is not a precursor to acute illness, and is undetectable with diagnostic equipment, sufferers are usually told they simply have to live with it.

Hypnosis stands alone as the most significant long-term solution for IBS symptoms. IBS hypnosis has been researched for over 20 years, and the results are consistently positive. The success rate for the relief of IBS symptoms through hypnosis ranges from 70-95% and relief usually lasts for years without the need for additional treatment. (IBSHypnosis.com)

The largest research study to date followed 250 IBS clients who were treated with 12 hypnosis sessions over a three-month period of time. The participants also listened to daily home reinforcement sessions. The patients showed dramatic improvement in all IBS symptoms. The average reduction in symptoms was more than 50%. Patients in the study also showed an improved quality of life and relief from anxiety and depression. (Gonsalkorale, WM., 2002)

Another study compared 25 clients with severe IBS treated with hypnosis to 25 patients, with similar symptom severity, treated with other methods. The hypnosis group had, in addition to significant IBS symptom improvement, fewer doctor visits, fewer work hours lost to illness, and an improved quality of life. Hypnosis clients who were unable to work before treatment were able to resume employment when the sessions were concluded. This study showed the economic and psychological benefits of using hypnosis to treat IBS. (Houghton, LA., 1996)

My IBS program involves six sessions spread out over a three-month time period. Clients rate their daily symptoms on a scale of one to ten, so that we can objectively track their progress. To give you an idea of how effective IBS hypnosis is, the average combined symptom rating at the beginning of sessions is eight; at the conclusion of sessions the number is three.

Many IBS clients have suffered for decades, but after a few short months, they learn to create peaceful comfort from within. With the help of hypnosis, they are able to replace anticipatory anxiety with the expectation of relief. When an individual knows they can use their thoughts to control how they feel physically, a wave of lasting relief usually follows.

DEIDRE'S IBS RELIEF

Deidre was a very unhappy 9-year-old girl. I initially saw her just two months after she was diagnosed with IBS. She had been suffering with pain, gas, and intestinal irregularity throughout most of her school year, and missed many days as a result.

Once Deidre's physician made the diagnosis, and explained that there was little in mainstream medicine that could bring her significant relief, Deidre's mother took action. She quickly decided that hypnosis was Deidre's best bet.

It is sad to see any child who is sick, but Deidre had two factors working in her favor. The first was her age. Children do extremely well with hypnosis. To them, it is like a trip to Disneyland. Their fertile imaginations easily supply the imagery and sensations that support their goals. Secondly, Deidre was pursuing hypnosis for a condition that can be relieved 70-95% of the time. Even though Deidre and her mother were unsure of the outcome, I was confidently looking forward to how well she would do.

After gathering all the information I needed, we shifted our efforts to the hypnosis session. As with all of my pediatric cases, I invited Deidre's mother to stay with Deidre during all her sessions. Usually, parents of children 12 years old and younger stay with their children during the sessions. Teenage children usually go solo, and most actually prefer it that way.

At the conclusion of the session, which runs about 10 minutes for children, Deidre emerged from hypnosis with a wide-eyed grin.

She expressed her amazement at the colors and fantastic imagery. She was also surprised by how good she felt. Prior to the session, she rated her stomach pain a six out of 10, and at the conclusion of the session, her pain was completely gone.

Throughout the remaining five sessions, Deidre made use of many hypnotic images that supported symptom relief, such as a team of imaginary healing specialists spraying her entire digestive system with a warm comforting solution, a control room that enabled Deidre to turn down unpleasant symptoms and turn up sensations of control and relief, and a video screen showing her how healthy and happy she was soon to become.

Deidre excelled during each visit and was able to experience 100% symptom relief. She loved listening to her home sessions, and also became very skilled with self-hypnosis. I occasionally receive emails from Deidre's mother with updates about her continued success.

Especially with children, hypnosis stops fear and uncertainty in their tracks. Children enjoy the ride and quickly integrate the helpful information of the sessions. Plus, they love the experience so much that they listen to home sessions with unparalleled commitment.

IBS HYPNOSIS SESSION

One of the most consistent problems IBS sufferers deal with, besides the actual symptoms, is the anticipation of symptoms. Most have been struggling for years or even decades, and have become conditioned to expect problems. By constantly dreading the recurrence of symptoms, their fear becomes a self-fulfilling prophecy.

With hypnosis we can break the cycle of anticipated symptoms by using a technique that empowers the individual to forget in a very productive way. Once people release images of themselves experiencing the problem, they can replace them with images supporting healthy success. Here is an excerpt from one of my IBS sessions:

As you continue integrating all that you hear, see, and feel with what you already know, you will begin to notice that you are becoming more mindfully aware of the benefits of hypnosis. Perhaps the sound of these words is more obvious to you; maybe it seems as though my voice is a bit louder at times, or maybe you are becoming more aware of certain sensations or emotions, or perhaps it's the many positive thoughts, and healing images, which resonate much more deeply than before.

Just as hypnosis can enlarge and magnify the way we perceive ourselves, it can also reduce or minimize whatever unproductive thoughts, memories, or emotions serve us best. We can take what was once emotionally or physically over-whelming, and reduce it, or even eliminate it from our day-to-day awareness, creating amazing new freedom and relief.

We can learn to forget just about anything. It happens every time we forget one thing or another. Sometimes it's an accident and other times it's no accident at all. Sometimes we choose to forget unpleasant situations, or we might forget about difficult assignments or responsibilities.

If we spend a lot of time fretting and worrying about certain problems, the subconscious mind is tricked into thinking that it is supposed to create what we're worrying about. If we dwell on a problem, we start to anticipate it or expect it to occur, and then it usually does. Over time, we can make a problem much bigger or more serious than it really has to be.

So today you will learn how hypnosis can give you the power to release and forget. As of right now, you have full authority to release any and all worry, stress, and concern about your symptoms of IBS. You have my permission to let go of anything and everything associated with it. Your subconscious is directed through hypnosis to relieve you of any and all unproductive patterns, emotions, and all of the unproductive worry of the past, easily and completely.

Now I'd like you to create an image of a computer screen in your thoughts. On the screen, create an image representing what your IBS problems might look like to you. It can be anything at all. Give this image of your IBS problem shape and color; define exactly what the symptoms would look like to you. Make the image very clear; even create a little uneasiness as you look at this image.

You know the saying, "out of sight out of mind." Here is a perfect example of what it means. Look down at the computer keyboard below the screen and imagine you can see a bright red button labeled "FORGET." Press it and watch the IBS image on the screen instantly disappear. It is gone, and as a result you feel a surge of freedom and relief.

Once again picture your IBS problems, but this time imagine that the Computer monitor is the size of a movie theater screen, so that the problem image is more enormous than you could ever imagine it being. The larger and more ominous you make the image, the more relief and freedom you will experience when you make it disappear.

Now hit the "FORGET" button again; instantly the image is gone. And after a little practice of repeating this technique, you'll begin to notice that you start to forget what the image looks like, and what it feels like. Because it's such a good idea for you to release everything related to your IBS problems, and because your subconscious mind can help you achieve this goal, it does, easily and productively.

Notice now when you try to re-create the image of the problem on the large computer screen, it's just a dotted out-line with no color. Now press the "FORGET" button again and it's gone. Now watch what it looks like when you try to create it again; there are just a few dots scattered about the computer screen, making no image of anything at all, and of course you quickly press the "FORGET" button and the dots instantly disappear.

Now one last time, try to re-create the image of the problem on the screen. Notice how you really have to work at it, but nothing appears on the screen; it remains completely blank. You have forgotten all about whatever it was you were trying to remember. Now, as you begin to understand the power and control you have, begin to use your creative freedom to envision a new, positive image of your healthy resilience.

Fill the screen with thoughts and images supporting the symptom-free life that awaits you. Create all the joy and fulfillment; fill it with color and all the details of your healthy success. Not only do you experience these positive thoughts or images, but now you begin to feel all the freedom and joy becoming real within you.

You have forgotten exactly what you chose to forget. You released the negative memories and replaced them with all the healthy joy you can Imagine. So now, in order to keep these positive changes locked in place so you never have to worry again, look down at the keyboard and imagine there is a bright green "SAVE" button, and press it; that's excellent. Now this enhanced application of symptom-free success is permanently downloaded into your powerful subconscious mind, supporting your lasting, healthy wellbeing.

PAIN RELIEF

I see many clients who have chronic, unnecessary symptoms of pain. The reason I refer to it as unnecessary is because many times the body uses pain as a way to signal us that something needs to be fixed. Examples would be infections, fractures, or even something like appendicitis. So anytime a potential client calls me for help with pain, I ask them for their primary physician's contact information so I can get his or her consent to try hypnosis.

Hypnosis enhances the mind-body connection so thoughts can positively affect the physical self. When chronic pain sufferers learn hypnosis, and understand that, with their thoughts, they can lessen the severity and duration of pain, they go from feeling like victims to experiencing sensations of control.

Individuals with long-standing, chronic pain also have difficulty with stress and anxiety, which often play a big role in creating or exacerbating symptoms. In fact, prior to all of my sessions, I ask clients if they have any minor, nagging discomforts such as headaches, aching joints, or tightness in the neck and shoulder area. If so, as we proceed with the session, I direct the flow of hypnotic comfort to saturate that particular area. At the conclusion of the session, the discomfort is usually gone.

Prior to a pain-relief hypnosis session, I ask my pain clients to rate their level of discomfort on a scale of one to ten, with one being no pain and ten being extreme pain. Let's say, for example, that the individual rates their pain as an eight. Once in a hypnotic state, I then ask them to imagine the pain scale and to focus on the eight. Then, by having them focus on a lesser number, I direct them to perceive a decreased sensation of pain. By using this simple direction during hypnosis, the mind begins to match the reduced sensation of pain with the lower number.

Once clients have reached a lower number, I'll guide them to focus on a number below that, and repeat the process. As soon as they reach a sensation of comfort, I usually suggest that they locate the imaginary lock button next to the scale. By pressing the button, the client will maintain their improved level of comfort.

Another effective approach for reducing pain is to have the individual focus on a pain-free part of their body, and then to mentally splash that location with one of their favorite colors. Then I guide the client to imagine the painful area in their body as another color. With both colors established, I then have them imagine that they are getting a comforting massage, and that the attendant is using a healing gel designed to change the color of the painful area to the color of the pain-free area.

Hypnosis can also assist individuals to create a unique perception, as though they were looking down at themselves, receiving the massage. Once this point of view is established, I ask them to see the color of the painful area starting to change. It can be a gradual process, but eventually the area of discomfort becomes the same color as the pain-free area. With the change in color comes relief.

The process of hypnosis provides additional benefits for clients suffering from chronic pain, because it releases endorphins, which are the body's naturally occurring, feel-good chemicals. This explains why most individuals experience a state of euphoria after a hypnosis session. During a session, individuals can also regulate the flow of endorphins, which provides them with another important tool in managing pain. Something as simple as an imagined control dial can put them in charge of their own comfort. Endorphins can be used both systemically or targeted toward a particular area.

With just a few office visits, most clients quickly master the hypnotic process, and rapidly become self-practitioners, able to enhance their comfort and become more relaxed, centered, and content.

One example of how hypnosis can help with chronic pain was demonstrated during a study of 42 migraine sufferers. These test subjects, all of whom had responded poorly to conventional treatments, were split into two groups. One received hypnotherapy to relieve their daily headaches; the rest acted as a control group. The hypnotherapy group experienced reduced frequency and duration of headaches. Intensity dropped by about 30%. "These results are impressive in such a difficult, hard-to-treat group of patients," commented Egilius Spierings, M.D., Ph.D. director of the headache section division of neurology at Brigham and Women's Hospital. (Gutfeld, G. and Rao, L., 1992)

ANDREA FINDS COMFORT WITH HYPNOSIS

Andrea was a 32-year-old professional woman referred to me by her primary physician. She had recently had back surgery to free up a restricted nerve that was causing her a lot of discomfort. Her surgery was marginally successful. Although her sensation of pain was reduced, she said it still interfered with her sleep and limited what had previously been an extremely active lifestyle.

Andrea described her job as one that required constant motion. As a sales rep, she did a lot of traveling and was on call 24/7. The financial rewards were enormous, but during the last few years, she had enjoyed her job less and less. I also learned during our initial conversation that Andrea was brought up in an athletic family; her father was a high school track coach who tried to instill his demanding views on fitness in his family. When she wasn't working, Andrea was a long-distance, competitive runner. In addition to all of her other stress, she had recently gone through a divorce.

We talked a lot about Andrea's lifestyle, the surgery, and how things were marginally better after surgery. I then asked her if she was happy. She didn't understand what that would have to do with the pain. I explained that what we think about most on a day-to-day basis has a significant effect on how we feel physically, emotionally, and even on the types of situations we draw into our lives. I also added that apparently there was a physical component to her pain which surgery seemed to improve, but that there could also be an emotional component still in need of attention.

I told her about a sixteen-year-old boy who had come to me for irritable bowel syndrome (IBS). He was not progressing with hypnosis as I thought he should, so during a session, I asked him to look forward in time, and see himself free of IBS. After the session, he said he couldn't envision such a scenario. He said everyone knew him as the kid battling IBS and that it was part of who he was.

In a subsequent session, I asked him if his healthy self would be able to help his IBS self make a transition. This is called parts therapy, and can be very effective in resolving inner conflict, which often leads to relief. After our work together, his symptoms began to subside. After hearing his story, Andrea was intrigued, and excited about pursuing hypnosis.

In her first session, I helped her learn how to deeply relax, and to also stimulate the flow of endorphins. When she returned for her next session, she was experiencing some relief, but still had a way to go. During the session, I asked Andrea what she thought the source of her remaining discomfort might be. Surprisingly, she was quick to respond. She said she hated her job and always had. Her father was in sales and he had pushed her into doing the same. She also hated running and maintaining her family's ridiculously high fitness standards.

I asked her what changes might increase her comfort level. She said her first move would be to find a job she was passionate about and also to start listening to and caring for her body, rather than punishing it with endless exercise. She also said that because hypnosis made her feel so good, she would continue practicing self-hypnosis.

At the conclusion of the session, Andrea was very emotional. She finally realized she had been driven for a long time by someone else's values. She was also amazed by the immediate, dramatic freedom she experienced. Many people who are looking for help are convinced that they know exactly what their problem is. Often, however, by using hypnosis to peel back the emotional layers, clients connect to their inner truth. Frequently hypnosis sheds new light on very old problems.

After a couple more visits, Andrea's pain was gone, and she was excited about her future. She still wasn't sure what professional path she might take, but she was considering all possibilities. She also certainly knew that happier days were coming.

SPORTS HYPNOSIS

Tiger Woods began seeing hypnotist Jay Brunza at the age of 12 for hypnosis and mental training. (SportsHypnosisWest.com)

Ken Norton used hypnosis to defeat Muhammad Ali in the 1973 fight in which Ken was a 7-1 underdog. Ali began using hypnosis soon after. (SportsHypnosisWest.com)

In 1984, Time magazine reported that Mary Lou Retton used hypnosis to prepare for the L.A. Olympics and to block pain in her injured foot to win the gold medal. (SportsHypnosisWest.com)

Since the subconscious is where all patterns and memories are stored, sports hypnosis is the only tool that enables athletes to enhance their performance from the inside out. If an athlete goes to the physical gym to improve strength and endurance, why not visit the mental gym to improve one's view of success?

In spite of investing a lot of money for lessons, studying the mechanics of their swing and watching endless videos, many golfers come to the point at which they no longer feel they are improving. Not until they include their mind in the training regime will they be able to take the next big step forward. Sports hypnosis optimizes the mind-body connection. This is a crucial step in maximizing athletic potential. Most golfers experience occasional moments of brilliance. With sports hypnosis, they mentally rehearse their success, so it can be replicated and consistent.

Mental imagery is a common technique in the sporting world. Sports hypnosis simply takes this concept to a deeper level of awareness. Hypnosis not only helps golfers feel like winners, but they can "experience" success before it occurs. For example, during a hypnosis session, golfers see and feel the ultimate drive and the tournament-winning putt. They can also create a visual path of light automatically guiding the ball to the cup. In addition, hypnosis can be used to focus the golfer's thoughts, thereby reducing or eliminating distractions.

Here is a great example of how one single event changed the perception of so many. On May 6, 1954, Roger Bannister had thoughts of running a mile in less than four minutes, an achievement that had never been done before. Not only did he succeed, but he opened the door for 45 other runners who accomplished the same feat over the course of the next eighteen months. It started with a single thought. The physical capability of the runners had not changed; what had changed was the belief that it was possible.

Researchers have examined the effects of hypnotic intervention on flow states and golf-chipping performance. The results support the hypothesis that hypnosis can improve golf-chipping performance and increase feelings and cognitions associated with flow. (Perceptual & Motor Skills. 2000)

CHUCK'S HOOP DREAM SUCCESS

Chuck was a high school junior who played on the basketball team. His goal was to be a starting forward. He knew he had the skills, but always came up short on the aggressive front, especially when the game was on the line. In the gym, he was a rebounding machine, and always dove across the floor for loose balls. At practice, his nickname was "madman." What propelled Chuck to pursue hypnosis occurred during one of the team's games, when he overheard a teammate refer to him as "madam" instead of "madman."

During Chuck's first office visit, he described how, during the team's practice, he would go into "the zone." All that mattered was getting the ball. During game-time situations, however, he was tentative, playing not to lose rather than playing to win. I suggested to Chuck that it was great that he didn't need to learn how to be a winner in game situations. He just needed to compete with the same intensity he displayed during practice.

I asked Chuck to describe the practice during which he had been most dominant. He said it was when he was asked to fill in during a varsity team practice. When he entered the scrimmage, some of his senior teammates gave him a hard time because they didn't think he belonged there. Once the action intensified, Chuck caught an elbow to the head while going for a rebound. He knew he was being challenged, and he passed the test. For the next two hours, he put on a rebounding clinic. From then on, he was able to carry his newfound confidence into every practice, but not into games. He felt as if he had stage fright. He spent more time thinking about the people in the stands than the opponents on the court.

During the first hypnosis session, I guided Chuck to re-create the confidence he felt during practice. Once he accomplished this, I had him imagine holding a magnifying glass over the image. I asked him to focus on the image until he felt a surge in his confidence level. Then, I asked him to imagine he could inhale the confidence, mobility, and skill he experienced at the practice. I suggested that he could breathe it in so deeply that it would reach a cellular level, and begin to replicate within him.

As he imagined how great he felt, I directed Chuck to visualize a door at the end of a gym. I told him that this door would lead him into the middle of a playoff game and as soon as he stepped through it, he would hear his name over the public address system, announcing his insertion into the game. His team was trailing by one point, with only five seconds left on the clock, and the opposition was in bounding the ball.

In this scenario, Chuck got to carry all the confidence he had just created into the game. With hypnosis, he had the unique opportunity to compete as the practice "madman" in the most important game of his life. I told Chuck that the instant I snapped my fingers, he could walk through the door and the game would continue, and in the silence of his thoughts, he was to imagine the outcome. I then snapped my fingers, and gave him a couple of minutes of silence to envision the results.

At the conclusion of the session, Chuck was ecstatic. He described how he was able to leap in front of the opposing player, intercept the in bounding pass, and complete a full-court pass to his team-mate, who scored the winning shot with no time left on the clock. He detailed the post-game celebration, how he was mobbed by his teammates, and the cheering fans who rushed onto the court.

Chuck felt as if a major barrier had fallen, and that he could confidently move forward. The remaining two sessions involved techniques that enabled Chuck to erase any remaining self-doubt, ensuring that he could routinely perform at the same high level he had imagined with hypnosis. He was also taught how to use self-hypnosis to re-create these empowering thoughts and images any time he wished.

Chuck was a starting forward for the rest of the year and also made the all-star team. Self-doubt limits our expectations and accomplishments. Hypnosis can help us understand that the only limits are those we self-impose. Hypnosis is the fastest, most effective way to break through barriers and claim our true potential.

WART RESOLUTION

Warts are caused by the human papilloma virus and there are many ineffective remedies for them, one as extreme as burning them off. Traditional interventions are like weeding your garden by clipping the weeds off at ground level. It looks good for a while, but they always grow back.

When I first heard that hypnosis could make warts disappear, I was more than skeptical, but when I learned about the physiological reasons as to why it works, it made perfect sense. At the time, I had already had success with irritable bowel syndrome hypnosis, and knew how powerful the mind-body connection was. It didn't take me long to design a program that has consistently produced positive results.

My initial focus for wart resolution is on stress reduction. If we are asking the body to heal from within, it is more able to do so when it is calm and peaceful. Another session supports enhanced immune response. Due to the viral nature of warts, a person with a strong immune system is more able to overcome the problem.

I also focus on circulation. With hypnosis, the client's circulation can be redirected so that the area surrounding the warts experiences a limited flow of oxygen and nutrients. This approach essentially starves the warts, causing them to dry up and disappear.

These techniques, combined with imagery assisting clients to see themselves as being wart-free, enhances the overall effectiveness of the program. As with any hypnosis treatment, home reinforcement is key. The seeds of success are planted during the initial office sessions, and by routinely visiting the empowering depths of hypnotic trance, individuals are able to bring about lasting relief.

In one study, 17 people with warts were hypnotized for a series of five sessions. Another seven people were not hypnotized and were instructed to abstain from using any wart remedies on their own. Three months later, more than half of the hypnotized group had lost at least 75 percent of their warts. The people who hadn't been hypnotized still had their warts (Owen Surman MD).

ERIC'S WARTS DISAPPEAR

Eric was a 12-year-old with dozens of warts on the back of both hands, as well as on his elbows and upper arms. His pediatrician referred him for hypnosis because he and his family had tried everything else. Many in my field are tired of always being the last resort for people, but I rather enjoy it. When an individual has exhausted all mainstream options, they tend to feel a little desperate, not knowing where else to turn. I think this type of client does better than most because they are highly motivated, do their homework, and want to change things in a hurry.

Eric's mother went over the details of the problem and I explained the process of hypnosis to both of them. After she left the room, Eric confided that his biggest worry was that his warts would scare away the girls.

Throughout Eric's sessions, he constantly heard about the drying process, and how the warts were no longer receiving adequate blood flow, thereby minimizing nutrients and oxygen. I also told him that, as a result, he should expect the warts to dry up and disappear.

He came back for visit two proudly showing me that his warts were becoming dry and flaky. Each session he went into hypnosis more easily, more deeply, and much more quickly. He also became very adept at using the words he heard to create dramatic images to support lasting, wart-free success. Traditional modalities only treat the symptom, which is the wart. Hypnosis is a point-of-cause treatment, which means it addresses the problem, not the symptom.

By Eric's third office visit, his warts were nearly gone. On his fourth and final visit, all that remained was the residual white discoloration where the warts had once been. Eric's mother dropped me a note a year later saying that the warts never returned and that Eric had a girlfriend.

ARTHRITIS RELIEF

Osteoarthritis (OA) is one of the oldest and most common forms of arthritis. Known as the wear-and-tear arthritis, OA is a chronic condition characterized by the breakdown of a joint's cartilage. Cartilage is the part of the joint that cushions the ends of the bones and allows for easy movement. The breakdown of cartilage causes the bones to rub against each other, causing stiffness, pain, and loss of movement in the joint. Over 27 million Americans have OA. (arthritis.org)

Stress plays a big role in exacerbating how one copes with OA, and communication is an important part of managing stress. The type of suggestions and imagery I use in my arthritis hypnosis program encourages the individual to verbalize what they are experiencing, which enables them to off-load concerns and frustration, which in turn reduces symptoms of stress.

Arthritis can also interfere with the quality of sleep. The deeply relaxing quality of hypnotic trance can be a welcome relief. If the hypnotic message an individual hears at bedtime supports deep, restful sleep, then that is what usually occurs. To have a quality life, one needs consistent, quality rest. Arthritis sufferers often experience difficulty just keeping up with the pace of day-to-day life. Constantly focusing on what they can't do only exacerbates the situation.

My arthritis program helps the individual recalibrate their day-to-day efforts to a more appropriate pace, and to also release any frustrations associated with perceived limitations. Rather than constantly struggling to achieve what is beyond one's grasp, I guide clients to shift their attention to what they can comfortably achieve.

Another helpful approach to arthritis is to incorporate regular exercise into one's lifestyle. By reducing body weight and increasing muscle tone, an individual can minimize the burden to affected joints, which increases mobility and comfort. Hypnosis makes it easier for a person to embark on low-impact exercise regimes such as walking or swimming. It also helps individuals create visions that support the improvements they want to make.

As previously mentioned, hypnosis stimulates the flow of endorphins. By learning how to use hypnosis to enhance endorphin production puts the comfort control back in the hands of the client.

Another unique aspect of hypnosis is how it can alter one's perception of the location of the discomfort. For example, it can be extremely helpful to redirect sensitivity away from key areas of the body, such as hips, knees, and vertebrae, and direct it to a less critical part of the anatomy, such as a fingertip.

I use the same approach to alter the quality of pain. For example, hypnosis can reshape the perception of a sharp pain to one that is dull, or hot pain can be perceived as cool. Another technique is color therapy. An example of this would be to ask the client to choose a color to represent pain, and another color to represent comfort. During the hypnosis session, the individual is guided to blend the two colors together, forming a new color. The new color allows increased control of comfort.

In a similar fashion, numbers can be used to reduce the perception of pain. As numbers decrease, so does the pain. Numbers are similarly used to guide individuals into hypnotic trance. I might say, "With each number you feel yourself becoming more and more relaxed, and by the time I reach the number one, you will be comfortably settled in hypnotic bliss."

HYPNOSIS IN THE HOSPITAL

Prior to becoming a hypnotist, I worked as a registered nurse. My acute care experience included an extremely fast-paced, general medical department and an angioplasty unit. I learned firsthand the hardship, stress, and grief so many of these patients endured. Once I became trained as a hypnotist, I realized how beneficial hypnosis could be in the acute care setting.

If the rapid assembly line of the mainstream health care system has clinicians increasingly overwhelmed, what about the physical and emotional state of those being cared for? What expectations do they have for recovery? Do they see themselves as temporarily side-tracked or powerless? Is there a role for them to play in their own recovery, or do they leave their health and wellbeing in the hands of others?

The authoritarian approach of western medicine assumes that health and wellness come from others. This belief minimizes the importance of our own natural ability to not only enhance our healing process, but to avoid illness to begin with.

Here are some applications of hypnosis in the acute care setting:

> *Intensive care*: Hypnosis helps patients block out distractions and increase their level of comfort, which improves quality of sleep and speeds up recovery time. It also reduces stress and safely balances blood pressure and heart rate, which helps minimize complications.

Hypnosis can also be used to reduce secretions and bleeding, optimize immune response, and also make medical procedures more tolerable.

Oncology: Hypnosis lessens anxiety, pain, nausea, vomiting, and reduces respiratory distress. It increases confidence and self-image, and also eases the patient's resistance to physical restrictions. In addition, hypnosis can be helpful in managing end-of-life transition.

A study of women with metastatic breast cancer showed that those receiving hypnosis over a one-year period were able to reduce their pain by 50%. In a 10-year follow-up, the treatment group had a survival rate of 36.6 months, compared to 18.9 months for those who did not receive hypnosis. (*Jour. of Behavioral Medicine* 1983)

Pediatrics: What better gift to give a frightened child than control during a time of crisis? Children have active imaginations and respond positively to hypnosis. Hypnosis melts away fear and increases relaxation and focus, making it easier for them to understand instructions, procedures, and treatments.

Mental health: Hypnosis relieves symptoms of sadness, fear, phobias, and addictions. It puts clients in control. They get to play an active role in their own recovery, which adds to an increased sense of involvement and ability to establish positive change. Everyone feels better about themselves after a hypnosis session.

Surgical: Pre-surgical hypnosis reduces anxiety, pain, stress, and bleeding. It promotes rapid healing and improves immune response. Surgical hypnosis helps the individual manage post-op pain and nausea, use less pain medication, and lessen the side effects that are often associated with some medications. Those who are positive and relaxed while entering anesthesia are positive and relaxed emerging from it.

These three studies highlight the benefits of pre-surgical hypnosis:

1) A more rapid return of post-op intestinal motility: 2.6 days vs. 4.1 days for those who did not receive hypnosis; length of hospital stay: 6.5 days vs. 8.1 days and an average savings of $1,200 per patient. (*Western Journal of Medicine.* 1993)

2) Patients in the hypnosis group had significantly less vomiting—39% compared to 68% in the control group—less nausea, and less need of analgesics postoperatively. Preoperative hypnotic techniques in breast surgery contribute to a reduction of both postoperative nausea and vomiting, and postoperative analgesic requirements. (*Acta Anaesthesiol Scand.* 1997)

3) In one of the earliest groundbreaking, surgical hypnosis studies, in the mid 1840's, John Elliotson and James Esdaile began using hypnosis in the surgical setting as an anesthetic. Prior to their efforts, mortality rate was 40%; with hypnosis it was 5%. In spite of their success, hypnosis would soon take a backseat to ether, nitrous oxide, and chloroform. by the late 1840's. (Inst. For Study of Healthcare Org. and Transactions)

ELSIE'S SURGICAL SUCCESS

Elsie was in her early 70's and was scheduled to have a benign mass removed from her left lung. She had no prior experience with hypnosis, but based on the recommendation from her surgeon, she was willing to give it a try.

The initial pre-surgical hypnosis session is designed to eliminate any worry or stress, and enhance trust in the surgical team. If the individual feels as though they are in good hands, they can spend more time focusing on healthy success.

Session two deals with the client's physical preparation for surgery. It directs optimum endorphin production to support postoperative comfort, and minimize stress. Session two also optimizes the individual's immune response, which minimizes risk for infection. Lastly, this session includes suggestions supporting ideal circulation, oxygenation, and proper absorption of medications and anesthesia.

Enhanced circulation minimizes bleeding, and carries healthy levels of nutrients and oxygen to areas that need them most. By directing proper medication and anesthesia absorption, the body is more able to take what it needs and secrete the rest.

All change begins with a thought, and with pre-surgical hypnosis, the most important seeds to plant support positive thoughts and images of postoperative success. Pre-surgical hypnosis session number three guides the client to perceive the surgery as though it were in the distant past. Elsie envisioned walking the beach with her husband, going to genealogical meetings, and spending time with her children and their families.

By entering surgery with a solid foundation of perceived success, the mind and body work together to create that vision. We are all familiar with clichés such as "what goes around comes around," and "be careful what you wish for." If there weren't an element of truth in these statements, they would never have become clichés to begin with.

Elsie's surgical experience was smooth and without any major complications. The nursing staff frequently commented on how quickly she recovered, and also how short her length-of-stay was, compared to others who had undergone the same type of surgery. Elsie embraced hypnosis from the beginning, and her diligent approach to home sessions clearly paid off.

There was, however, an interesting bump on her road to recovery. I happened to be in the hospital, and stopped by Elsie's room a couple of hours after her surgery was completed. Coincidentally, I entered the room as the nurse was encountering a problem with the intravenous pump that was administering Elsie's pain medication. The hospital staff realized the pump had malfunctioned, and needed to be replaced. As a result, for a short period of time, Elsie was not receiving pain medication.

As I chatted with Elsie, the nurse left to get a replacement pump. I could see her facial expression changing; she was grimacing in pain and soon became tearful. Knowing that relief was on the way, I asked Elsie if she wanted to use hypnosis for relief. She readily agreed. In seconds, Elsie went from whimpers of pain to comforting, hypnotic relaxation.

During the session, I told Elsie that if she wanted to remain in this comfortable daydream for the rest of her hospital stay, she could. I suggested that when she emerged from hypnosis, she would be responsive and alert, but it would feel like a dream and that anytime she wanted to increase her level of comfort, all she had to do was to gently rub her thumb and forefinger together. This simple gesture would instantly create the relief she desired.

The session only lasted about ten minutes and Elsie was alert and comfortable when the nurse arrived with the replacement pump. She was surprised to see how relaxed and at ease Elsie appeared to be. When she asked Elsie for an explanation, Elsie said, "My hypnotist took care of everything."

Once the pump was in working order, I asked Elsie if she wanted to go back into hypnosis again, only this time I would allow her to remain there as long as she chose. She liked that idea. Once in hypnosis, I reinforced her ability to glide through the rest of her hospital stay in her dream-like bubble and also reminded her to use the finger rubbing technique anytime she wished to enhance her comfort.

Several days later, Elsie called my office to report that all went well. She said that after I left her room, she slept comfortably throughout the night, and awoke the next day, pain-free. She had required only a minimal amount of pain medicine throughout the night and was cleared for discharge the following day.

REGRESSION HYPNOSIS

Regression hypnosis is one of the most fascinating applications of hypnosis because it offers profound insight into times earlier in or even prior to the client's current life. The primary clinical benefit of regression hypnosis is to assist individuals to go back in time in order to resolve a problem at its point of origin.

For example, a client presented to me with unrelenting leg pain that did not respond to medical treatment. During a regression session, he journeyed to a prior life in which he suffered a traumatic injury, requiring amputation of the leg. The reason he still carried the pain in his current life was because he never learned the lesson that the past event was intended to teach him.

During a regression session, it is helpful to explore the events of another time, and to help the client understand what transpired. Then, with a better sense of the past, I can help a client separate the past moment from his current life. The process can be as simple as cutting an imaginary cord, which then propels the client forward into a life free of the burden of the past.

Throughout our current and past lives, we can get stuck in emotional potholes. Hypnosis is therefore an extremely productive tool, enabling an individual to learn what needs releasing or repairing. Clients suffering for decades can walk out of the office, after one regression session, feeling completely free. A recent example of the mainstreaming of regression hypnosis came in May of 2008. Oprah Winfrey dedicated an entire program to regression hypnosis with renowned hypnotist Brian Weiss, M.D.

JOE'S JOURNEY

Early in my practice, I had a client, Joe, who presented with relationship problems with his partner. He was reluctant to commit to a long-term relationship, which caused stress in the relationship. He wanted to know why commitment was so difficult for him.

During the regression session, he went back hundreds of years, and saw himself as an infant carried in a basket. He was left at the door of strangers who cared for his physical needs, but there was no love. I helped him understand that what he saw as abandonment could very well have been the ultimate act of love. I suggested that his parents might have believed that by giving him up to others, he would be safe. I also helped him to disconnect from any perceived negative aspects of this memory, so he could be free to go forward.

This session actually had a couple of regression stops along the way. After Joe's initial regression, he made a second stop. This time he journeyed to an earlier point in his current life. As a young boy, he was scheduled to have minor surgery. For whatever reason, his parents chose not tell him about it. Instead, they just dropped him off at the hospital. Even though his stay was brief, and the procedure was successful, he was traumatized by the event.

To help smooth out this memory, we accounted for the era: it was the late 1940's, when family communication was often limited. He also said that his parents never spoke much to each other, or to their four children. Taking these details into consideration, I suggested that Joe now had the opportunity to hold onto memories of value, and he could release the rest. Simple, rational interpretations might seem trivial to the conscious mind, but during hypnosis, they can represent the missing ingredient to lasting relief.

During Joe's session, I pointed out that his current real-life difficulties were influenced by his memories of the distant past. I suggested that all of his life memories added together were too numerous to count. During hypnosis, I asked Joe if he thought it was a good idea to place those two particular memories into the pot with all the others. He agreed. Then, I suggested that when he did so, he would experience instant relief. I gave him a few moments to accomplish this simple task. Then I concluded the session by asking him to begin envisioning his new freedom from the past and how it would translate into a more meaningful relationship with his girlfriend.

During our post-session conversation, Joe was amazed at how good he felt. He described feeling as though a weight had been lifted from him. Weeks later, I received an email from Joe saying that his relationship had significantly improved.

HOW TO SELECT A GOOD HYPNOTIST

In most states, hypnosis is not a regulated profession, which means that anyone can take a weekend seminar, and call themselves a hypnotist. With this in mind, it is a good idea to do your homework when considering enlisting the services of a hypnotist.

The first step would be to find someone who is also a licensed healthcare provider such as a physician, registered nurse, psychologist, psychiatrist, or a social worker. Because these individuals are formally educated and licensed in their particular field, they are more likely to offer professional quality care.

Although most doctors know very little, if anything, about hypnosis, you might also ask your primary care physician for a referral. Another resource would be holistic health centers, where there are usually several modalities under one roof. In this setting, there is more likely to be a collective professional atmosphere, which might ensure a more competent hypnotist.

There are also several reputable organizations such as the National Guild of Hypnotists (NGH.net) and the International Association of Counselors and Therapists (IACT.org). These organizations usually have a referral network. You can also do a quick Internet search for hypnotists in your area. A practitioner's website should offer helpful information such as office rates, qualifications, specialties, and you can also get a feel for their level of professionalism by how they present themselves on their website.

During your initial phone conversation, you can determine if the hypnotist is generally interested in your situation, how long he or she has been in business, and what their qualifications are. You can also inquire if they are affiliated with any national organizations, if the hypnosis session(s) will be specific to your needs, whether the hypnotist teaches self-hypnosis, and if you will receive a recording of the session for home reinforcement. You should also inquire how many sessions are required and if they offer references. I have a long list of satisfied clients who are eager to share their experience with prospective clients.

Unfortunately, there are many poorly qualified practitioners in the field of hypnosis who do very little in terms of preparing you for long-term success. Rather than empower you, they prefer to have you keep coming back for costly office visits.

If you get all the right answers, and feel good about the hypnotist you are speaking with, the last thing is to make sure their rates are in line with the geographical area they practice in. This varies greatly from one part of the country to the next. If you feel good about how the hypnotist presents him or herself, don't let a few dollars get in the way of a positive experience. For example, the average cost per session in the Greater Boston area ranges between $125-$150. If you still aren't sure if it's a good fit, ask if the hypnotist offers free consultations. I have offered them since I opened my practice and it is an excellent way for the client to determine whether or not hypnosis and the practitioner is a good fit for them.

Once you have chosen a hypnotist and scheduled your first appointment, the last hurdle is to decide if you will be comfortable in their office setting. As is the case with psychotherapists, hypnotists can practice in a professional building or out of a home office, and there are pros and cons with each. I started out working from a home office, then opened a second office in a professional building, and a year later went back home again.

You will know right away if the hypnotist's office is clean, quiet, and professional in appearance. The hypnotist should make you feel welcomed and cared for. There should also be a comfortable place for you to sit or lie down during your session. If everything meets your approval, relax and prepare to enjoy the experience.

HYPNOSIS ON THE TUBE

Early in my practice, I had the opportunity to be a guest on a local cable TV talk show, where I explained the process of hypnosis and did a short demonstration. Two years later, I attended an open house for alternative practitioners, and a local chiropractor was talking about a cable program he hosted, and how much it helped his business.

The next day I contacted my local cable access station to inquire about starting my own show. A few days later I had a volunteer crew, a set design, and programming ideas. Once the show, Healthy Hypnosis, was up and running, my priority was to expand the viewer base by promoting it in other towns. Most communities only require a signed sponsorship form by a local resident, for the show to be added to their schedule. During the next three years, Healthy Hypnosis rapidly grew and is now seen in 45 Greater Boston communities. It is also being uploaded by cable stations nationwide.

During the show's infancy, I thought it would be difficult to produce ongoing hypnosis-related programming, but I was pleasantly surprised. The first thing I learned was how eager every hypnosis practitioner was to come on and share their views. I also invited referring physicians, nurse practitioners, and past clients to appear on the show. The clients are my favorite guests because nobody knows better than they how effective hypnosis can be. In addition to telling their success stories, many agreed to participate in hypnosis demonstrations. The demonstrations are very helpful for showing viewers what to expect.

One of my early programs featured an 85-year-old woman who was dramatically successful in relieving her symptoms of irritable bowel syndrome. Speaking in a distinct British accent, she eloquently described how she quietly scoffed at the notion of hypnosis prior to coming to see me, and how after her first session, she was a believer. She had a total of six sessions and months later appeared on the show, completely free of her IBS symptoms.

Another dramatic guest appearance was a woman in her thirties, who originally thought she was coming to see me for weight loss. After a couple of sessions, she had an epiphany. She realized that she could use hypnosis to peel away years of depression and connect to her true inner self, which she did in dramatic fashion.

She spoke at length about her past values and beliefs, and how she thought she needed to navigate through life. Helen had been on medication for depression for years, and began to rethink that as well. It is important to understand that it is never the role of a hypnotist, ethically or legally, to make recommendations about medications or medical treatment. When the subject came up, I suggested that she consult with her primary physician. After doing so, she safely came off her medication while staying committed to daily hypnosis sessions at home.
Her appearance on the show took place four months after her final office visit to my office. She was eager to come on the show to share what she had learned about hypnosis, and how it can offer dramatic clarity and relief in the most unexpected of ways.

Another client was scheduled to have gastric bypass surgery but decided to check out hypnosis first. Once he learned about the possible surgical complications, he also realized that it was not a miracle cure. He understood that surgery would do nothing to change the deeply rooted, unhealthy patterns that caused the excess weight to begin with.

During his appearance on Healthy Hypnosis, he described how quickly he noticed things changing after his first hypnosis session. He felt as if he had options and began to make better choices. Over the first couple of weeks, he also noticed that he was easily losing weight. After years of struggling, he finally was taking control and was eager to share his story with the viewers.

I believe that practitioners in the field of hypnosis not only have a responsibility to offer quality work, but also to educate the public and to advance the general acceptance of hypnosis by mainstream society. For too long, hypnosis has been forced to lurk in the shadows of myth and misinformation. I made the commitment early on in my practice to advance the cause, and Healthy Hypnosis has become an extremely effective, enjoyable way to spread the word.

HISTORY OF HYPNOSIS

Descriptions of the hypnotic process go back 6,000 years. During the past 200 years, hypnosis has become more formalized, but has had to battle against organized religion and medical science for mainstream acceptance. Here is a chronological listing of some of the most significant leaders in the field:

Franz Anton Mesmer (1734–1815) The Austrian physician is commonly referred to as the father of hypnosis. His technique was called animal magnetism, which he claimed involved the individual's psychic and electromagnetic energies. Even though his work was shunned by the medical community, it was Mesmer who was responsible for spreading the word of the soon-to-be-called hypnosis to the newly settled United States. This is how the term 'to become mesmerized' originated.

In 1784, the French Academy of Sciences, led by Benjamin Franklin, was commissioned to evaluate Mesmer's technique. They concluded that he was not the one doing the healing, but that his patients were actually self-healing. They said that the patient's imagination was enhanced with Mesmer's technique, empowering them to become completely self-healed. On the surface it seemed that Mesmer was labeled a failure. Actually, the commission proved what we have all come to learn about the true nature of hypnosis; that all hypnosis is actually self-hypnosis.

James Braid (1795–1860) was a Scottish physician who coined the name hypnosis, which is a Greek derivative of the word for sleep. Braid soon realized that hypnosis was not sleep at all and later unsuccessfully tried to change the name to monoeidism.

James Esdaile (1805–1859) was a Scottish surgeon who moved to India. He successfully performed 345 major operations, using only hypnosis as the anesthetic. Soon after his dramatic research was published, ether was discovered, replacing the need for hypno-anesthesia.

Jean-Martin Charcot (1825–1893) was a French neurologist who labeled the three stages of hypnosis as lethargy, catalepsy, and somnambulism.

Pierre Marie Félix Janet (1845–1947) was a French neurologist who advanced the use of hypnosis for the therapeutic value of relaxation and healing. He was in the minority of those who used hypnosis during the growing popularity of psychoanalytic therapy.

Sigmund Freud (1856–1939) claimed to not prefer hypnosis be-cause he thought he couldn't hypnotize patients deeply enough. It was also commonly known that he had poor hypnosis technique. Freud's shunning of hypnosis slowed its acceptance by the medical community.

Milton Erickson (1901–1980) was a Nevada born psychiatrist who is commonly referred to as the father of modern hypnosis. He was the master of indirect hypnotic suggestion. He played a significant role in the 1958 acceptance of hypnosis by the American Medical Association.

Made in the USA
Middletown, DE
02 August 2017